The Impossible Revolution?

STUDIES IN SOCIOLOGY

Consulting Editor: PETER I. ROSE *Smith College*

The Impossible Revolution?

BLACK POWER AND THE AMERICAN DREAM

Lewis M. Killian   *The Florida State University*

RANDOM HOUSE
New York

To my children Kit, Lew, and John,
with the wish that their world
will be better than I predict.

Foreword

In *Hogan's Goat,* an off-Broadway play about Brooklyn in the late nineteenth century, the Irish hero proudly proclaims, "When I stood in the landing shed of this 'promised land' I made a vow. I'd fight my way to power if it killed me. Not only for myself but for our kind."

Today, in Brooklyn and elsewhere across the nation, young Negroes are echoing similar sentiments. They, too, are vowing to fight their way to power. Yet there is a difference in both the tone and the tempo of their protest: the tone is bitter and the tempo frenetic.

Negro youth have been taking to the streets in increasing numbers, defying both the obdurate white community and those older Negro and white civil rights leaders who have been trying to win the battle for equality without bloodshed. Tired of promises of things to come, bitterly frustrated by ghetto-living, sweltering in the oppressive summer-city heat, and seething with a hatred born of denial, they are seeking action—and many are seeking revenge. While many of their spokesmen proclaim, "We don't want to get whitey; we want to get him off our backs," they argue that the Negro masses must close ranks and unite under the flag of Black Power.

Of course not all Negroes have taken up the banner. Indeed, many, perhaps even the majority, are frightened at the most recent turn of events. And yet there is little doubt that sympathy for the sentiment underlying the new rhetoric touches all who are black in white America. Even middle-class Negroes (and their ranks are steadily growing) well appreciate the appeal of their "brothers." They and the "Negro respectables" who belong to the steadily employed working class find themselves on the horns of a profound dilemma, caught between the group with which they are invariably identified and those whose aspirations they share. But they are not the only ones confounded by the new militancy.

It is not at all uncommon today to hear many well-meaning white people, including the children and grandchildren of European immigrants, self-righteously contrasting their struggles with those of Negroes. They say that they had to fight their own way out of the East Side of New York, or the South Side of Chicago, or the slums of Boston, or some other tenement district by their own efforts and without the help of special programs or special agencies; and that they did so without disrupting the society or getting "The Man." Many point out that in the old days only hope and a belief in the American Dream were needed to spur them on. Though quick to forget the problems *they* encountered —the waves of anti-foreign sentiment and the blatant and subtle forms of discrimination—and the political intrigues in which *they* engaged in order to overcome the label, "greenhorns," the fact is that the majority of immigrants *did* manage to make it and eventually found successful accommodation in the new environment. But it is also true that opportunities for Europe's immigrants, even the desperately poor, were far greater than any ever afforded colored peoples and, especially, Negroes. As economist John Kenneth Galbraith is reported to have quipped, "If you have to be born poor, at least have the good sense to be born at a time when everybody is poor."

This is only part of the problem. Not only are southern Negroes entering the urban economy at the wrong time according to the

Galbraith dictum, but unlike most American minority groups, they have not had much to look forward to and even less to look back upon. Negro Americans have shown little of the interdependence and fellowfeeling of the Irish and the Jews and the Chinese and even of the Puerto Ricans. Rather, they have been united by the stigma of color and the strain of persistent relegation to second-class status. Many—and perhaps most—Negroes have tended to see themselves as whites have seen them, as persons to be disdained and ashamed of. They have internalized the white definition of their place in the society.

The signs advertising American egalitarianism have always read FOR WHITES ONLY. It is a brutal fact of life for one-tenth of our population. Negroes have long stood (and continue to stand) on the outside looking in. In many ways they are aptly called "marginal men." Although they may dwell in the inner core of our great urban centers, they remain on the metaphoric margin, apart from, not a part of, the wider society. To this day for the majority of Negroes in this country, the Dream is still deferred.

The late Langston Hughes once asked the rhetorical question, "What happens to a dream deferred?" Does it "dry up like a raisin in the sun," "fester like a sore," or "crust and sugar over" —or does it "explode"? Negroes have reacted in each of the ways posed by Hughes' metaphors. Through acceptance, flight, or imitation, many capitulated, "sagging," as he put it, under the heavy load of discrimination. But there was an explosion too—one whose fuse runs a long way back in American history, back to the days of Frederick Douglass.

From the welter of programs advanced by Negro leaders in the late nineteenth and early twentieth century, two themes became dominant. One, in the tradition of Booker T. Washington, advocated self-help and internal organization; the other, following the lead of W. E. B. DuBois, stressed integration and civil rights.

As Washington's program of accommodation eventually turned into one of militant pride and nationalism (by such chauvinistic groups as the Garveyites and the Black Muslims) and DuBois' plan for concerted legal action increasingly turned to extra-legal methods for tearing down the color bars (by such integrationists as those in the NAACP and the Southern Christian Leadership Conference and, for a time, the members of CORE and SNCC), each sought the support of the Negro masses. Neither ever generated enough to bring about dramatic changes within or outside the ghettoes; changes sufficient to break the back of segregation. In fact, until very recently most Negroes remained too intimidated to act; whites, too recalcitrant or too indifferent to care about changes.

With the Supreme Court's school desegregation decisions of 1954 and 1955, many Negroes felt that at long last America's promise might be their own as well. But as is all too apparent today, the elation was premature. Despite the legal gains and the far-reaching civil rights legislation that followed, the majority of Negroes did not directly benefit. The years of relegation to inferior status, of denial, of outright persecution had taken a great toll. Though desirous of "Freedom Now," many Negroes were not truly prepared for it; nor were the majority of white people. As Kenneth Clark has said: "the so-called Negro has been robbed of his identity, marked by oppression and then proclaimed incapable of integrating with whites." The removal of legal barriers did little to alleviate the basic malaise that pervaded the black neighborhoods and the souls of black people. It did serve to demonstrate the depth of racism. A new term, *"de facto segregation,"* became part of the vernacular. The southern whites' long-denied charge that northerners, too, were segregationists at heart seemed to be vindicated by the increasing backlash phenomenon.

To stem the tide of frustration and increasing bitterness, some

Negro leaders tried to join the bifurcated themes of pride and protest. What some first called "the Negro revolt" was an attempt not to overturn the society but to join it. But after a decade of struggle most Negroes remained marginal, remained beyond the fringe of acceptance. Therefore it was almost inevitable that without dramatic changes alternatives would have to be sought to the strategies that led to the Pyrrhic victories of the late 1950s and the early 1960s. Radical leaders soon came to the fore asserting that they were tired of having their people beaten and vilified in sit-ins and freedom rides and protest marches where only *they* turned the other cheek. And with often convincing arguments, they began to proclaim that the new laws served more to assuage the guilt of the white liberals than to serve the cause of the ghetto-dwellers and tenant farmers. "Brotherhood" was supplanted by the new slogan, "Black Power." The change in the battle cry signaled the significant changes now occurring in character, focus, and leadership of the struggle.

The character is changing from the demand for "Freedom Now" (which, for many, came to mean jobs for which only certain individuals were already skilled; housing for which a small minority could already pay, etc.), to the recognition of a poor people (a poor and black people—a double stigma in the wider society) who not only know they are poor and black, but know precisely what this means and what their needs really are.

The new focus already means introspection as well as greater militance. "Negritude," "soul," or whatever euphemism is used, is becoming predominant. Until about 1963 the major thrust of most of those at the forefront (and in the field) of the movement was essentially "whitewardly mobile." Today, many members of the new generation of Negro leaders have changed their emphasis; some have changed their entire course. Now, to coin a phrase, they are "turning blackwards." The late Malcolm X once said, "the worst crime the white man has committed has been to teach us to hate ourselves." Across the country, in city after city, the Negro is being exhorted to assert that he, too, is a man, a somebody.

The shift toward increasing chauvinism is being greeted with ambivalence even within the wider segment of the Negro population, with indignation and hurt in many white liberal circles, with mounting fear by many others. And its most extreme manifestation portends an ever increasing expansion of destructive behavior as those who live in Harlem and Hough and Newark and Watts are exhorted to give "whitey" his comeuppance. Yet for others the new ideology provides the basis for the establishment of a sense of pride and community that has been lacking.

As pride in being a man—in this case, a black man—increases, leadership changes too. In the civil rights movement (or, at least, what is left of it), whites are being eased (and sometimes pushed) from positions of leadership to make room for Negroes, who can identify more easily, and be identified, with the masses of black people.

The real question that remains is whether the new turn of events will facilitate genuine and relevant community organizations with power to alter the status quo of segregation, or whether the "Second Reconstruction" will end in tragic failure like the first while the so-called Negro Revolution becomes a series of violent, self-destroying rebellions.

Those intellectuals who take the former position are quick to invoke the model offered by other minority groups. They say that in essence Black Power is not an attempt to destroy society but a basis for pride and representation to those lacking it; the same pride and recognition that the English, the Italians, the Irish, the Jews, or the others have had in themselves. It is also the basis for the formation of institutions that can implement organized actions and concerted and coordinated programs to aid in the ascent up the ladder. Those who believe this to be the case suggest that the "ethnicity" that already exists among Negroes must be strengthened, and ethnic power (Black Power) must become a factor to reckon with. They say that this is really nothing new—it is as American as apple pie!

But there are others who are not so certain the analogy is apt. Lewis Killian, the author of this volume, is to be placed in the ranks of those who do not believe that the current phase of the Negro Revolution signals a new beginning. To Killian, and to others, these events may be tolling the death knell of Negro advancement. In *The Impossible Revolution?* Killian relates the history of the American Negro's attempts to come to terms with his status. He documents and describes the ebb and flow of the civil rights movement and the reactions of Americans—white and black, northern and southern, conservative and liberal. With poignancy and penetrating insight he lays bare the depth of incipient racism that pervades the society to this day. He also describes the nascent reaction to it by the newest group of Negro spokesmen —those who advocate Black Power.

Killian's diagnosis is profound; his prognosis is dire. Negroes, he argues, suffer in a manner unmatched by any other ethnic group, and whites have done little to alleviate that suffering. The society itself is viewed as the source of the disease, and Black Power is seen as a desperate but misdirected attempt to eradicate the cancer of racism that affects this country.

What Killian fears most is the inability of Negroes to translate their language of estrangement into a meaningful remedy that will cure the disease without killing the patient. Indeed, he feels there is no easy way out of the present dilemma. Old techniques have failed because they didn't help those who needed help most. New techniques (as advocated by Stokely Carmichael, H. Rap Brown and others) will fail, he says, because they will inevitably alienate the white Establishment which is most needed in abetting the transition.

The Impossible Revolution? offers no solutions. Such is not the author's intention. He is not unmoved by the trauma he describes; he is simply unwilling to offer the kind of easy panacea that almost inevitably greets the reader in the final chapter of books such as his own. Killian is utterly honest; and he is profoundly sad.

Perhaps in time he will be proven wrong. Perhaps beneath the surface of the calls for "creative violence" there *is* a profound awareness of the necessity to come to grips with the dual problems of self and community plaguing Negroes, problems clearly elucidated by Professor Killian and alluded to above. Perhaps it is still possible that a people may not only learn to say, "We're somebodies too," but will also be able to create those institutions necessary to develop new leadership and bloc unity.

It must be said, however, that given the current pattern of race relations in the United States such a program is not easy to implement without substantial help from outside; for there is little likelihood that Negro Americans can succeed alone. The anguished cries for help must be acknowledged. The "power structures" in cities across the land must begin facing up to their responsibilities for redressing grievances, rather than continuing to offer palliatives to restore the peace after the lids have blown. But will they?

The chasm between the white majority and the black minority yawns wider with each summer of discontent. The urban caldrons continue to seethe, anarchy continues to supplant disciplined nonviolent direct action and, as Killian asserts, the future does not look very promising.

Peter I. Rose

Northampton, Massachusetts
July 1967

Preface

This is a pessimistic book, but the times are ominous. After years of racial crisis we are brought to a grim realization of how deeply the roots of racism have extended into American society. The racial problem grows not out of the soil of individual prejudice, but out of the very social structure itself. No matter how much white Americans may deplore the cruder forms of discrimination and the more obvious consequences of prejudice, they are not likely to make the sacrifices needed to change the fact that America is still a white man's society. The theme of Black Power reflects the growing disillusionment of Negro Americans with the white man's willingness to give up his position of supremacy. This theme is not new. Almost a century ago Frederick Douglass warned that the Negro's liberty must depend upon his own power rather than upon the goodwill of white Americans. The crisis facing the nation is one of power; of Black Power, in all its forms, versus white power.

The sociologist, no matter how gloomy his predictions, is usually inclined to end his discourse with recommendations for avoiding catastrophe. There are times, however, when his task becomes that of describing the situation as it appears without the consolation of a desirable alternative. There is no requirement in social science that the prognosis must always be favorable; there may be social ills for which there is no cure. Therefore, this book has no happy ending. Reluctantly the author must state his honest conclusion: there is no way out.

My thanks are given to James M. Fendrich of the Florida State University for his careful reading of the manuscript and his many helpful suggestions for its improvement. I am equally indebted to Peter I. Rose of Smith College, the Consulting Editor, for his valuable advice and, particularly, for the time he took from his busy schedule to expedite the publication of this volume. I am grateful to Suzanne Kinderman and Mary Smith for the cheerful spirit in which they performed the tedious task of typing the manuscript. Michael Pearson, who someday will be a sociologist in his own right, made my task easier by his work as my research assistant. My wife, Kay, deserves more than the usual thanks for patience and moral support. She actually read the book in preparation, and her enthusiastic reaction to the early chapters encouraged me to see the work through to completion.

L. M. K.

June 1967

Contents

Contents   xx

The Impossible Revolution?

The Impossible Revolution?

By standards of common sense it seems impossible that the most depressed tenth of the population of a highly industrialized, democratic nation could, without arms or outside support, embark on a revolution. Yet, the phrase "the Negro Revolution" has become part of the present-day language of the United States.

Of course, the meanings of dramatic phrases are notoriously elusive, as elusive as the varied motives of the phrase-makers. After all, do not the glib writers and commentators of the highly competitive mass media label almost any newsworthy social change a "revolution," from changes in the attitudes of adolescents to changes in the styles of automobiles? Certainly, many of our conceptual tools have been devalued by the hyperbole characteristic of the market in words.

It is not even clear how seriously those who speak of the Negro Revolution take their own words, nor is it certain when the term first came to be used. After the student sit-ins of 1960, Louis Lomax began to use the phrase "the Negro *Revolt*" to call attention to the shift in tactics from legalism to direct action. In 1962 he published a book under this title.[1] In 1963, the editors of *Newsweek* launched a study of the attitudes of Negro and white Americans toward civil rights and the racial crisis. The results were published in a volume by William Brink and Louis Harris entitled *The Negro Revolution in America*.[2] They specified, however, that this was a *social* revolution.

When Robert Penn Warren interviewed Negro leaders in 1964 for his book *Who Speaks for the Negro* he asked many of them, "In what sense is this a revolution?" [3] The answers seemed to emphasize the *non-revolutionary* nature of the revolution. Roy Wilkins, of the NAACP, replied, "We are not seeking to overthrow a government or to set up a new government. We are here trying to get the government, as expressed by a majority of the people, to put into practice its declared objectives." [4] Martin Luther King, Jr., declared that this was a new kind of revolution. "This is a revolution to get in. . . . Revolutions have been centered on destroying something. Whereas in this revolution the quest is for the Negro to get into the stream of American life." [5]

In his book *To Be Equal* Whitney Young, Jr., of the National Urban League, makes explicit the reservations that many Negro intellectuals have about the phrase "the Negro Revolution" even when they use it themselves. He writes:

> This revolution bears little similarity, however, to the American Revolution or the French Revolution or to the Russian Revolution. There is no attempt here to overthrow a government. This is a revolution against historic injustice. . . . This is a revolution . . . to gain the rights and respect that should be synonymous with the word "American." It is a revolution not by black people against white people, but by people who are right against those who are wrong.
>
> This revolution is unlike others, also, in that, after three hundred years of deprivation, the deprived seek redress for their grievances in an expression of faith in a nation that has done very little to deserve and nurture such faith. [6]

While these leaders speak with, and of, revolutionary fervor, they seek to soften the harsh overtones of the term "revolution." If this is a revolution, it is not a revolution *against* any class, any race, or any government; it is only against evil, injustice, and prejudice. Only the ignorant would see any threat to the nation in it since its goal is to fulfill the national ideals, and the revolutionaries themselves have deep faith in the government. Furthermore, this is a revolution that has been distinguished by reliance on nonviolent tactics.

But some of the angry men of the movement have not shrunk from the more drastic implications of the word "revolution." James Farmer was hardly speaking of revolution figuratively when he analyzed the fusion of the pacifistic idealists of CORE with the indigenous anger of the Negro masses to produce a "revolutionary mass movement." He entitled his article, "The New Jacobins and Full Emancipation." [7] Unlike King, he views nonviolence not as "an inviolable spiritual commitment," but as a tactic which might be abandoned if it does not achieve its ends.[8] It is evident that he uses the label "New Jacobins" with an informed sense of its antecedents in the vocabulary of the French Revolution when he declares:

> What the New Jacobins demand today is total war to achieve total rights. If there is any word more hated in the struggle than "moderation," it is "tokenism." This revolution exacts from its revolutionists, and requires of its friends and allies, a staunch and thoroughgoing commitment in both motivations and concrete actions.[9]

The New Jacobins of whom Farmer wrote in 1963, and even newer radical leaders, are still the exception among Negro spokesmen in that they do not avoid the most extreme implications of the word "revolution." On the whole, however, Americans who speak of the Negro Revolution use the term loosely, not as a precise conceptual tool that would place the current crisis in the spectrum of types of social change. To most Americans, white and black, the Negro Revolution is still the Impossible Revolution.

· The Importance of a Name

The obvious question at this point is, "What's in a name?" Will what we call the Negro's struggle for full citizenship change the nature of its course? Will not observers continue to call it the Negro Revolution without worrying about what they mean, or even while denying with the next breath that it really is a revolution? How, in fact, can we tell whether a movement is a revolution until it is over?

It is indeed easy for students of history to identify social movements as revolutions after they have occurred. When a government has been overthrown or an attack on the ruling elite has been crushed, it is clear that a revolution has been attempted.[10] According to another criterion, a revolution may be said to have occurred when "the basic institutional (i.e., legally enforced) values of a social order are rejected and new values accepted." [11]

The overthrow of a ruling group or the acceptance of a new set of basic, institutional values represent, however, the final act of a long, historical process. In many revolutions of the past those revolutionaries who laid the groundwork for the eventual overthrow of a government had no such end in mind. It is typical in revolutionary movements, including the Negro Revolution, for the proponents to claim that *their* values are the basic or true values of the society. They do this even while their opponents are claiming that they are the guardians of the values that have always been the foundation of the social order. It is exactly such ideological competition in the current racial crisis that makes many Negro leaders seek to qualify their use of the term "revolution." They are only seeking to complete the American Revolution begun in 1776, they suggest; it is the white Establishment that has forsaken the basic American values. Hence, by the definitions suggested above the Negro Revolution is not really a revolution.

By yet another definition, however, a revolution may be identified early in its development. This definition depends not on the outcome of the movement but on the means that the movement is forced to use because of the response of the larger society to its demands. A revolution is not an incident that occurs at a dramatic point in time. It is a mode of action developed by a group of people as they seek to change their position in society and, in doing so, encounter certain kinds of opposition. A revolution is a social movement that comes to be regarded by a significant portion of society as *dangerous*, that is therefore opposed with force, legal and illegal, and that thereby is compelled to rely on illegitimate means to achieve its objectives.[12] Blocked in their initial efforts to improve their condition by working within the existing structure of the society, participants in a social movement may begin to question the validity of both this structure and the values that justify it. Thus the movement becomes a revolution that challenges both the authority of the ruling class and the legitimacy of traditional values. A distinguishing feature of such a movement is that it attempts to create fear, not favor, in the public.

By this last definition, the Negro protest movement has become truly a revolution. Recognition that this Impossible Revolution is indeed possible may serve as an antidote to the apparently irrepressible optimism about the racial crisis in America. This is the sort of optimism that finds hope for an early and peaceful solution to the crisis in every court ruling narrowing the boundaries within which segregation may be legally maintained, in every increase in Negro voting, and in every new federal program that promises to make middle-class Americans of the Negro masses. It is an optimism that denies that Stokely Carmichael, Adam Clayton Powell, and the rioters of the ghettoes have become part of the mainstream of the Negro protest movement. It is an optimism that leads, in spite of dire warnings, to the belief that Negro Americans will cling indefinitely to their faith in the American dream. In the years since the fateful decision of the Supreme Court in 1954, countless highly placed statesmen have reiterated the theme, "American Democracy is color-blind!" Given such a noble ideal plus American ingenuity in social engineering, there should be no need for a revolution to give Negroes the feeling that they are at last first-class citizens.

· The Social Framework

It has been suggested that the term "Negro Revolution" is usually used with tongue in cheek. One reason is that revolutions are just not supposed to occur in the United States. Our country is a young nation in the company of great nations; yet, in less than two centuries, it has become the wealthiest and, probably, the most powerful nation of its time. Most important, it can rightfully lay claim to being the symbol of democracy. The revolution that brought it into being was the bellwether for uprisings against old monarchist and colonial regimes throughout Europe and Latin America; its constitution has been copied over and over by new republics. In contrast, the *novus ordo seculorum* of the young American republic was not copied slavishly from the model of nations with a very different history. The concepts of freedom and order were hammered out slowly over the period of a century, from the early struggles of the southern frontiersmen against the Lords Proprietors to the adoption of the Bill of Rights. While the colonists were always challenging the remote rule of proprietors, royal ministers, and Parliament in England, the American system was built on the firm foundation of the long evolution of democracy in England. The new nation was born with a history of striving to expand the boundaries of freedom. Although the nation is nearly two centuries old, its citizens believe that it is still dedicated to the original revolutionary goals of freedom and equality, not to the defense of entrenched privilege. According to this belief, another revolution should be both unwarranted and unthinkable.

The structure of government is also designed to make revolutions unnecessary. There is provision for orderly and regular change of government, contingent neither on the death of a monarch nor on a parliamentary crisis. Popular representation in the framing of laws is promised through the Congress, particularly through the lower house with its broad base and frequently shifting composition. In spite of centralization of government, individual citizens are given massive protection through the Bill of Rights and the federal judiciary. At the same time, much of government is kept close to home by the preservation of the autonomy of states, counties, and municipalities as powerful political entities within the union. The many parts of the complicated structure mesh in an amazing system of both horizontal and vertical checks and balances. Tension among the parts is constant and no concentration of power in any one part can long go unchallenged.

The most remarkable thing about the system is how well it has worked from the beginning. Although the federal government was born as a revolutionary government, its "reign of terror" was so mild as to be hardly recognizable as such. Although George Washington was both hero and first executive, he became neither king nor president-for-life. The nation not only survived the fratricide of the Civil War, but soon afterward moved into the ranks of the world powers. Despite the dire predictions of his adversaries, Franklin D. Roosevelt neither abolished presidential elections nor founded a dynasty. After weathering the Great Depression, America became the arsenal of democracy and the leader of half of the world. Extremists on the left gathered their largest following only when they attempted to make themselves indistinguishable from liberals during the Depression or from patriots during World War II. Native fascist movements have never been able to find the "man on horseback" behind whom they could unite, and overt anti-Semitism has never become quite respectable. There is little wonder that the theme "It can't happen here," vigorously attacked by Sinclair Lewis in the thirties, still retains its vitality.[13]

Yet the same characteristics of the American system that make revolution improbable also make it an ever-present possibility. The placid surface of consensus and orderly change conceals powerful undercurrents of dissent, conflict, and frustration. In speaking of the civil rights movement as part of "America's continuing revolution," the sociologists George E. Simpson and J. Milton Yinger observe optimistically, "In democratic societies, revolutions are always partial; and they are never completed. . . . This may prove to be the greatest social invention of man—the creation of a type of social system in which continuous adjustments can be made without violent destruction of the whole structure." [14]

Being pessimistic, however, one may observe that partial and incomplete adjustments may provide only palliatives, not solutions, for social inequities. The adjustments of the Missouri Compromise and the Compromise of 1850 did not prevent the unsuccessful revolution called "the War Between the States."

· The Lack of Consensus

The student of American values can readily find numerous citizens who profess belief in such slogans as "all men are created equal," "life, liberty, and the pursuit of happiness," and "with liberty and justice for all." But he can just as readily find those who violently disagree about the meaning of these phrases. Jane and Wilson Record make the point concisely when they observe, "The highly diverse, sharply conflicting nature of the American value context is often obscured by attempts to associate 'the American character' with a particular set of ethical traits." But, they add:

The American value heritage encompasses both the prag-
matic-prudential ethic and the moralist-utopian ethic. The
individualist-equalitarian strain is there, but so is the
groupist-conformist-elitist strain. . . . The consequent ethical schizophrenia has been noted by European students of
American life, from de Tocqueville to Myrdal, for more than
a century.[15]

Despite all the hallowed documents enshrined in the National
Archives, Americans have no sacred writings to spell out their national values for them. They have no Ministry of Truth to define
the meanings of the value-statements that they utter. Instead American values are at the center of a constant debate. Diverse and
ambiguous, they provide ideological support for the most diver-
gent practices and programs. With reference to the present crisis,
the Records observe, ". . . the American ethical heritage has been
sufficiently diverse not only to sustain the Negro in his alternate
needs for endurance and revolt, but also to nourish his oppres-
sors." [16]

· Checks and Balances

It may be argued that this diversity and ambiguity of values is a
luxury the society can afford because the structure of government
provides for continuous, orderly adjustments. The system of checks
and balances has prevented any prophet of true Americanism from
imposing his interpretation of these values on the whole society as
happens in totalitarian societies. It is not popular consensus as to
the meaning and the limits of freedom that provides the strongest
guarantees for the maintenance of freedom; it is the equilibration
wrought by the constant tension between majorities and minorities.
Thus change comes about not through bold strokes of emergency
action designed and executed by social engineers, but through a

long process of debate and compromise. Though the economists, the sociologists, the engineers, and even the military planners may propose, it is the politicians who dispose. Politics, rightly defined as "the art of the possible," can dull the cutting edge of the most finely balanced, sharply honed blade of social planning. It can reduce a coherent plan of reform to a package of inconsistent, even contradictory, "titles" in a law that finally resembles the plan chiefly in its name.

Whatever the output of the legislative process, the process itself is usually slow. When it has not been slow, as during the Reconstruction Congress and the "hundred days" of the New Deal, much of the product has failed to stand the test of constitutionality. Indeed, too often filibusters and committee inaction have delayed specific and significant pieces of legislation for decades after the need was first recognized and for years after popular support was extensive.

The judicial process, stretching back sometimes for years before a decision is rendered in the halls of the Supreme Court, can be equally lethargic. Justice delayed may be justice denied, but rarely are judicial decisions reached as quickly as the litigants feel they can and should be. Cases are concluded most speedily in city courts, but few would argue that the justice of the magistrates' decisions increases in proportion to the speed of their summary judgments.

Even when law has finally been made, either by legislative debate or judicial deliberation, the antiauthoritarian safeguards of the American system make its execution an uncertain affair. First, there is the diffuseness of the system of enforcement. The courts—particularly the federal courts—constantly strive to impose consistency in the interpretation and application of the law by the many different enforcement agencies. But thousands of police forces, from one-man departments to the Federal Bureau of Investigation, are facets of a prism that refracts the pure light of the law into a myriad of hues. In some corners of the nation, the light of the law of the land seems not to reach at all. In such areas, what purports to be a government of laws is in truth a government of men—of a poorly educated police chief, a venal justice of the peace, a power-hungry sheriff, or the representatives of an entrenched aristocracy.

· The Source of Freedom

This critique reveals the hard reality that it is not so much altruistic dedication to the ideals of freedom as it is the constant struggle of different individuals and groups to advance their *own* liberty and self-interest that has preserved the measure of freedom that Americans enjoy. The efficient orderliness of a coerced consensus and a planned society has been forgone for the sake of freedom. But this is a dangerous game. The freedom that is ever being bought is always unevenly distributed: there are always discontented segments of the population wavering between faith in the opportunity to secure their rights and disillusionment with the system. An even more remote, but graver, danger is that the pursuit of short-run gratifications by different interest groups may in the long run prove destructive of the whole system.[17]

The dangers inherent in the preservation of freedom through conflict are seen most clearly in the economic realm. Although it is nowhere spelled out in the Constitution, the tradition of free enterprise has always occupied a prominent place in the gallery of American values. That the American economic system has never been uniformly free has no more destroyed the vitality of the ideal than has the uneven distribution of political freedom vitiated belief in liberty. The system has been free, however, in the sense that economic interest groups have been able to fight unremittingly for their rights. It is now abundantly clear that what has evolved is not a nation of strong, independent merchants, manufacturers, farmers, and laborers, each protected equally in economic freedom by a government that penalizes only dishonesty. Instead, massive politico-economic blocs wield considerable influence over production, prices, employment, wage rates, and credit, and thereby influence the whole economic machinery. As the power of big business, organized labor, and associations of farmers has grown, the involvement of government in the economic system has expanded until it, too, has reached gargantuan proportions. Much expansion has been fostered by the wielders of economic power themselves. Some has come at the demand of "little people," who have found that only through their votes can they defend their economic interests in this uneven competition.

The concentration of power in massive corporations, lending institutions, and labor unions leaves large numbers of citizens exposed and defenseless in the no-man's land of the economic battle. The small business man, the small farm owner, the farm laborer, the unskilled and unorganized worker, and the pensioner find their freedom, their opportunity, and their security limited by their lack of power.

The uneven distribution of economic power is accompanied by an uneven distribution of wealth. Recently, attention has been drawn to the fact that the United States faces the paradox of unprecedented affluence for the majority and poverty for a not-so-small minority.[18] The irony and the tragedy of the paradox are heightened by the realization that the prosperity of the many makes the poverty of the few both less endurable to the poor and less visible to the affluent. The affluent majority, predominantly white, speed on the freeways past these pockets of poverty. It is difficult for these affluent people to visualize the plight of the inhabitants; the poor remain anonymous and unreal to them. It is even more difficult for them to believe that a revolution might be brewing in the ghettoes.

· **It Can Happen Here**

Disbelief in the possibility of a real revolution has thus been sustained by three things. The first is the belief that the political system rests on a firm foundation of a consensus of basic democratic values. The second is the remarkable flexibility and resilience of the political structure that, except between 1861 and 1865, has enabled it to maintain its coherence and continuity in spite of crises and internal conflicts. Finally, there is the contemporary ability to disregard burgeoning poverty so completely that the War on Poverty had to ride in on the coattails of the racial crisis.

Yet these same factors may carry the seeds of a genuine revolution. The ethical diversity underlying the mask of consensus could provide the ideological ammunition for a revolutionary movement as well as for a counterrevolution. The flexibility of the political structure and the limitations on power also limit the capability of the government to respond speedily and decisively to crises created by new needs. The inability of the affluent majority to perceive the crisis of poverty-in-prosperity does not mitigate the desperation of the millions of poor people. Instead, it exacerbates it.

No segment of the American people has felt the impact of all three forces more keenly than have the twenty million Negro Americans. Rich or poor, they have experienced the ethical schizophrenia of the nation in their daily lives and are intensely aware of the diverse practices that American values may be invoked to support. The only minority group for whose protection three constitutional amendments have been added, they look back over a century of disillusionment with the efficacy of law as a panacea. And all the variables which are related to economic deprivation meet in disproportionate frequency in the Negro population.

If a Negro Revolution or any other revolution should come

about in the United States, it would take place in an unusual context. The faith that democratic values inspire, as vague and diverse as these values may be, would give such a revolution a distinctive character. In a society that is already supposed to be the embodiment of revolutionary and democratic values, it is difficult to draw the line between the old and the new, the revolutionary and the traditional. If they looked only at the professed values and the bold promises of society, even the most depressed group would ask only to be included; they would not demand that the ideals be changed.

Certainly in its early stages the Negro Revolution was defined by most of its leaders as an attempt to gain greater participation by Negroes in American society, not to change drastically the values and the structure of that society. This rested, of course, upon the assumption that this society is basically color-blind and that only certain interest groups have subverted it by emphasizing the theme of race. Examination of the nature of the Old Regime will suggest, however, that the theme of white supremacy has always been an integral and pervasive feature of the American system.

II

The Pressure for Revolution: The Old Regime

The nation that was to become the champion of democracy was conceived to the accompaniment of the eloquent, defiant phrases of the Declaration of Independence. Its birth was announced by the ponderous, legalistic articles of the Constitution. The Declaration enunciated principles of freedom and equality, which any man could acclaim so long as they applied to him and his kind. But the Constitution reflected a series of compromises between different constituencies that had developed as separate political entities and economic classes in the colonial period. Despite the inspiring principles of the Declaration and the loyalties born during the war against England, under the Articles of Confederation the conflicting interests of these constituencies had almost destroyed the nascent union.

Rather than proclaiming a new creed, the Constitution established a system of government. It was designed as a workable plan to establish order among states and interest groups that had already found the values of the new American creed amenable to many interpretations. The nation thus established has been described as "a society in a continual state of tension between action generated in various spheres and tolerated or reinforced or resisted by other organized groups and the state" [1]—a society displaying the sort of organic solidarity envisioned by the French sociologist Emile Durkheim.

This system of countervailing tensions has never produced a perfect balance of power between the constituent spheres. Despite the lip service paid to the principle of equality, not all men have been equal; not in politics, in economics, in religion, or in social acceptability. As the society has grown larger and encompassed more and more diverse groups, the referent of the term "all men" has become increasingly obscure. Traditional practice has conformed to the proposition that some men are more equal than others! In the political realm, as in the economic, the pattern of inequality has reflected the early history of the nation. Informally and unofficially an Old Regime has developed. The existence of this Old Regime was difficult to recognize until it was eventually challenged.

What is the nature of this Old Regime, which, despite the numerous changes in the society, still wields overwhelming power? In an acute analysis of the modern challenges to it, Alan P. Grimes characterizes this Old Regime and its sources. He declares:

> Traditionally, American politics has reflected in its principles the composition of its constituents. For much of our history, the country has been predominantly Protestant and has reflected in its politics a Protestant prejudice, for all the intended separation of religion from the political affairs of men; the country has been predominantly white and has reflected in its politics a pattern of white supremacy; the country has been predominantly rural and has reflected in its politics this rural hegemony.[2]

In spite of the growth of cities, of industrial empires, of giant labor unions, and of ethnic political machines, the dominance of the white, Protestant, rural-minded representative in the Congress has been evident throughout the nation's history. It has been even more evident in state legislatures. More significantly, the white, Anglo-Saxon Protestant remains the typical American, the model to which other Americans are expected and encouraged to con-

form.[3] Grimes' thesis is that three of the most notable and contro-
versial decisions of the United States Supreme Court in recent
years symbolize the long-delayed challenge of a changing society to
this heritage. These are the prayer in public schools case of *Engel
v. Vitale* (1962); the school desegregation decision in *Brown v.
Board of Education* (1954); and the legislative reapportionment
ruling in the case of *Baker v. Carr* (1962). In these cases the
new, growing constituency, "essentially cosmopolitan and urban-
oriented," has challenged the superiority in religion, race, and politics that the Old Regime has so long enjoyed.[4]

But the challenges to Protestant and rural dominance do not
manifest the revolutionary potential exhibited by the challenge to
white supremacy, although they augur extensive social change. The
battle-lines are not so clearly drawn, identities are not so difficult to
change, the threat to self-conceptions is not so profound.

· The Religious Challenge

True, the growth of the Roman Catholic and Jewish segments of
the population through immigration has destroyed the basis of the
assumption that this is a Protestant America. But the foremost
champions of a literal separation of religion from politics and national loyalty have been neither Catholic, Jewish, nor Protestant;
and the adherents of all three faiths have been sharply divided
about the issue. After all, they could rest assured that the God to
whom their children were to be required to nod before they started
the business of the school day would be left unidentified. Each
could privately believe that his particular definition of God was the
real one, and that only the rude or the fanatic would insist on
making an issue of the point. In the meantime, all could agree that
He looks with special favor on them because they are Americans.

That such an amorphous American God could come to be acceptable to Americans of so many denominations and faiths can be explained in terms of the nature of the religious establishment in the United States. As Will Herberg,[5] Ruby Jo Kennedey,[6] and Milton Gordon[7] have shown, the melting pot theory has worked, in a way, insofar as religion and nationality are involved. A triple melting pot has developed in which once harsh differences between nationalities and denominations are being dissolved and softened in three great religious communities. These communities are able to live in comparative peace with one another largely because Catholicism and Judaism in the United States have been modified in practice, if not in doctrine, in the direction of the Protestant American model. For many sincerely religious Americans, regardless of faith, God has become a spiritual dynamo who set the universe in motion; an ever-present comfort in time of trouble; and an ethical teacher who, it so happens, propounds those moral and spiritual values on which all respectable citizens can agree. So long as the American worships at the church of his choice and does not let his religious beliefs create awkward situations in his business or social relations, he is likely to be accepted as a respectable, loyal, God-fearing citizen.

It is for citizens who openly reject belief in a vaguely defined supreme being and for devout religionists whose beliefs inhibit conformity to the norms of other areas of life that religious freedom is a critical issue today. A small minority of devout believers and determined nonbelievers have succeeded through court action in stripping off from state-supported activities many perfunctory rites of what was becoming a state religion. They have forced the religious leaders of the favored faiths to rethink the implications of their dependence on the state, not only for moral sanction, but also for indirect financial support. They may succeed in stopping or even reversing the growth of subsidies of religious activities; it is unlikely that they will drastically change the structure or the culture of American society. For most Americans, religious convictions as distinguished from nondenominational moral and spiritual values simply do not have enough relevance to economic, political, and social activities to be decisive in shaping the culture. Nowhere is this more evident than in the current racial crisis. Both sides in the conflict use religion as a weapon; but the conflict is basically a secular power struggle and not a holy war.

· The Urban Challenge

Nor is the challenge of the urban majority to rural dominance likely to become revolutionary although it, too, may lead to extensive changes in the culture. The lines between the antagonists are not sharply enough drawn, nor are the divisions sufficiently stable. The rural and small town voters of one election may be urban voters in the next. Within a few years, a small county may become part of a big county complex through the expansion of a metropolitan region. Indeed, the shift to urban political dominance is almost a *fait accompli*, simply because of the size of the urban vote. Although the Supreme Court's insistence on equality of representation in the House of Representatives and in state legislatures has been vigorously denounced, and although the Court has been vague as to how equality is to be achieved, the size of the urban majority guarantees that the principle will not be overthrown. Compliance will be more than token, although concessions undoubtedly will be made to the rights of the rural minority. All that remains to be accomplished is the working out of the details of an accommodation between the new and powerful urban majority and the rural minority, which has only enough power to stage a brief delaying action.

Whatever the details of the accommodation, the result will be a new political alignment centering in the urban areas. Present trends indicate that the central city-suburban division will replace the old rural-urban dichotomy as the ecological basis for political alignments. And as Negro registration and voting increase even in the Deep South, the division along lines of color will have even greater significance than it has had in the past. If the Supreme Court extends the one man, one vote principle to county and city electorates, Negroes may find their political influence enhanced on the local level. Yet the reform measure of requiring the election of city councilmen "at large" rather than by district has already been developed to counteract Negro political power in some cities.[8]

· The Negro Challenge

It is the challenge to white dominance that will require the greatest adjustments in the social order and that possesses the greatest revolutionary potential. The lines between the two constituencies are more sharply drawn than in the case of religion or urbanism. Membership is involuntary and is extremely difficult to change. The division between the two sides of the conflict is supported by both social and physical distance. Wherever they live in any number, Negroes constitute a community within a community.[9]

The Negro challenge is not unrelated to the other two challenges to the Old Regime, even though it is different from them and more acute. Although most Negroes are Protestants, they have not been encompassed in the triple melting pot. Indeed, Negro Protestants constitute a fourth religious community, both in terms of institutional structure and in faith.

· The Negro and the Religious Challenge

Negro religion in the United States has not been a part of the American religion of which we have spoken. The Judeo-Christian ethic as interpreted by the great majority of white Americans has come to be identified as an integral part of the American way of life. The church as an institution has not only been supported by but has also given its sanction to the other major institutions of the society—business, education, and government. While a minority of intrepid clergymen and laymen have always played the prophetic role, the distinction between the kingdom of God and the city of man has been blurred for the majority. In his indictment of "the religious establishment," Peter Berger asserts, "The religious institution does not (perhaps, one should say 'not any longer') generate its own values; instead, it ratifies and sanctifies the values prevalent in the general community." [10] And speaking particularly of the "central core" of American Protestantism, he says, "Commitment to Christianity thus undergoes a fatal identification with commitment to society, to respectability, to the American way of life." [11]

Although Negro Protestantism has not avoided becoming a social religion, it has always stood in judgment on the American way of life in a way that white Protestantism, Catholicism, and Judaism have not. The formation of the separate Negro denominations after the withdrawal of Negro churchmen from white parishes was a condemnation of the white supremacy that had become an integral part of American culture. The other-worldliness that characterized Negro religion for so much of its history implied a rejection of the popular faith that America was the best of all possible worlds, the land of opportunity. During the outbreak of the present racial crisis, beginning with the Montgomery bus protest, the Negro churches made their condemnation of the status quo and of the social religion of the white churches explicit by demanding changes on "this side of Jordan." The Negro churches did not initiate the Negro protest movement, but when changes in the position and the aspirations of Negroes made the old, escapist religion unpalatable, Negro ministers were quick to alter their message. One of the first targets of their condemnation was the white religious establishment.

Negroes, whether Protestant or Catholic, have little stake in the specific issue of the involvement of the state with this establishment. They may, however, benefit from the weakening of white Protestant hegemony. Berger points out that even though Catholicism and Judaism have been strongly affected by the common faith of American cultural religion, they have not been part of the central core and have remained in a state of greater tension with the overall culture than has white Protestantism. It may even be argued that had the Roman Catholic church been stronger during most of the nation's history the course of race relations might have been significantly different. Frank Tannenbaum in his book *Slave and Citizen* has shown how the tension between the Catholic hierarchy and the secular authorities in Brazil led to the gradual abolition of slavery and forestalled the development of an ideology of white supremacy in that nation.[12]

· The Negro and the Urban Challenge

The challenge of the urban majority has greater significance for the Negro because he is a growing part of that majority. Ironically, during the long heyday of rural political dominance, Negroes were the most rural of Americans; but they shared no part in this dominance. In the South they could not vote; outside the South they were scarcely present in the rural areas. The growth of Negro political influence has closely paralleled the increase in urban power. Equality in representation for the urban majority, promised in *Baker v. Carr*, will result in even greater influence for the Negro constituency.

Still, until other aspects of the social structure are changed, this influence will continue to be reflected indirectly through a sort of proportional representation. As Negroes have flocked to the cities of the nation, residential segregation has resulted in gerrymandering, both accidental and deliberate. The flight of white residents to the suburban ring and the burgeoning of Negro ghettoes magnifies the separation of the Negro from the rest of the new urban majority. Conditions in the inner city, where he is concentrated, make his interests special and acute. When white voters want slum clearance, he asks, "Will there be more living space and better housing for displaced Negroes?" When white parents demand better schools, Negro parents ask, "Will they be integrated?" When the white power structure seeks to attract new industry, the Negro worker seeks assurance that it will provide employment for him. Every step which represents progress for the white segment of the urban majority carries a threat for the Negro segment, for it may mean that the gap between white "haves" and Negro "have-nots" is widened. And the Negro's political demands carry a threat for the white segment, for most of them entail an increase in the tax burden, as well as an end to the white man's monopoly of the better jobs, the better residential areas, and the better public facilities.

· The Racial Crisis

Typically a Protestant, the Negro remains a member of a segregated fourth faith. Increasingly an urban dweller, he is primarily an inhabitant of the central city with its desperate problems, of which he himself is one. Above all, he is still visibly a Negro, and he can change that identity only if he is able to "pass." The United States is ceasing to be a Protestant, rural nation, but it still remains a white man's country. The prayer decision and the reapportionment ruling confirmed and legitimated changes that had already been largely accomplished. The school desegregation decision of May 17, 1954, however, heralded the beginning of a long battle for an extensive reordering of the social structure, a reordering that had scarcely begun at the time. This crisis is the more acute because it has been in the making for so long a time. In Grimes' words, "The amicable accommodation of religious differences in America has been a significant achievement of our political experience; our inability to achieve a similar accommodation of racial differences has been our most conspicuous political failure." [13]

· The Heritage of White Supremacy

To assert that the United States is a white man's country is to open the door on a skeleton in the family closet. It is a truth that only the most disillusioned Negroes or the most prejudiced whites have been willing to state bluntly. It is not the message of the great historical documents of the nation, but it is the message of history.

From 1776 to this day, when white Americans have debated the status of the Negro, they have reached not consensus but an uneasy compromise. There is no question that many delegates to the Continental Congress, including southern statesmen like Jefferson, saw the contradiction between slavery and the theory of natural rights. But Jefferson's stirring words of condemnation of the slave trade were struck from the Declaration of Independence in order to insure acceptance of the document by other white delegates from the South. John Adams said of the first draft, "I was delighted with its high tone, and the flights of oratory with which it abounded, especially that concerning Negro slavery which, though I knew his Southern brethren would never suffer to pass in Congress, I certainly would never oppose." [14]

A minority of hard-core, proslavery southern delegates was present to frighten Adams away from a forthright statement on the Negro's stake in liberty. There could be no Negro delegates on hand to oppose this trading away of their dignity for the sake of unity between white Americans. Most Negroes were still slaves, and none were part of the body politic. This has been the story of the Negro in America. He has always had the moral support of a significant minority of white Americans who believed in his full manhood, but it has never been the part of respectable patriotism to suffer white unity to founder on the rock of the Negro's status. Even when the union was broken in 1861, it was the slogan, "Union Forever," not "Freedom for All," that rallied northern patriots to the colors.

· **Compromises in the Constitution**

Represented only by their white friends, not by spokesmen from their own ranks, Negroes have been unable until the present crisis to veto the compromises accepted by their sympathizers. The compromises embodied in the Constitution were even more disastrous than those made in the wording of the Declaration. Again the motives of the delegates to the convention were varied. There was some abolitionist sentiment based on recognition of the inconsistency of slavery with the idea of the rights of man. There was also considerable opposition to slavery stemming from fear of the growing size of the slave population. Some northern delegates were concerned lest the counting of slaves as persons for purposes of representation give the slave states disproportionate power. The southern delegates, whatever their feelings about the morality of slavery, saw in the slaves a tremendous financial investment and a supposedly unassimilable mass of aliens. A few delegates, notably those from Georgia and South Carolina, felt that their states needed more slaves. None of the southern delegates, however, could visualize Negroes living in their midst except as slaves.

Thus the abolition of slavery and the conferring of citizenship upon Negroes were not issues at the Constitutional Convention; the continuation of the slave trade was. The antislavery delegates would not allow this issue to remain unresolved. The compromise that was reached on the question of the slave trade and the one concerning the basis of representation in the House of Representatives were a white man's solution. The slave was treated as property. He became three-fifths of a man for purposes of representation and direct taxation. The slave trade would be permitted to continue for at least twenty years; and the Negroes, like other valuable articles of commerce, could be taxed at ten dollars a head. Citizenship being a matter for the states to decide, the political status of the free Negro was left undefined, but it was specified in Article IV that flight into a free state would not relieve the slave of his bondage.

Thus while the founding fathers did not openly declare that this was to be a white man's nation, and while many of them felt that it should not be so, their compromises for the sake of union made it possible for it to become exactly that. In the quarter-century following ratification of the Constitution, sentiment for emancipation grew even in the South, but so also did hopes for solution of the Negro problem through deportation. The formation of the American Colonization Society in 1816, with leading southerners such as Henry Clay, William H. Crawford, and John Randolph as members, reflected both a growing fear of slavery and an inability to imagine Negroes as free citizens. Colonization failed, however; the only place to export surplus slaves was to the new states coming into the Union in the west. The southern slaveholders had a double stake in the extension of slavery into the western territories. Each new slave state constituted not only a market, but also a bulwark against the power of the free-labor, industrial states of the North.

· Abolitionism and the Free Soil Doctrine

The developing abolitionist movement, particularly the eastern wing led by William Lloyd Garrison, was perceived as a threat and even more as an insult by southern slaveholders. The fulminations of the abolitionists against the immorality of slavery challenged the white southerner's conception of himself as a Christian, and led to the development of the ethnological argument as a philosophical defense of slavery. Yet radical abolitionism never constituted a respectable social movement even in the North. The radical abolitionists stirred up insurrection among the slaves, they threatened the Union with the cry "No union with slave-holders" and they denounced the Constitution itself as "a covenant with death and a league with hell." Garrison did not have to go to the South to be in danger; he was almost lynched in Boston.

The Free Soil doctrine was a much greater threat to southern white interests than was radical abolitionism. This doctrine demanded only that slavery be prohibited in the new territories being organized in the West. It conceded the constitutional right of the states to legalize slavery, but sought to stop the spread of the institution. Both Free-Soilers, like Lincoln, and southern slaveholders recognized that this policy carried the seeds of the destruction of the political power of the slavocracy and eventually of slavery itself. The Free Soil movement was respectable in the North where it advocated change by constitutional methods and was expressed in practical political maneuvers. It was one of the foundation stones of the new, but already viable, Republican party, which constituted the principal opposition to the badly divided Democratic party. The Republican party was beginning to show an ominous unity on the proposition that slavery should not be extended into new territories.

· Lincoln, the Union, and the Negro

By the middle of the 1850s, the nation was terribly divided on the issue of slavery, primarily, but not solely, on sectional lines. The spectrum of political views ranged all the way from the no nation without slavery of the southern slavocracy to the no union with slavery creed of the radical abolitionists. But the official position of the nation, arrived at in a perfectly constitutional manner by a majority of the United States Supreme Court in the Dred Scott decision, decreed that this was indeed a white man's country. Not only was the Missouri Compromise, limiting the spread of slavery by congressional action, declared unconstitutional, but the Negro was declared not to be a citizen. Lincoln's election on a platform that advocated the restoration of the Missouri Compromise, not the immediate abolition of slavery nor the conferring of citizenship on the Negro, was sufficient to frighten the southern radicals into secession. Yet Harry V. Jaffa in reviewing Lincoln's stance on emancipation says of him:

> He was the most conservative of antislavery men. He did not, in any campaign, urge any form of emancipation other than that implied in the exclusion of slavery from the territories. First privately, later publicly, he favored gradual emancipation, and in the plan he recommended to Congress in December, 1862, the state action which he envisaged might have been extended over thirty-five years, until 1900.[15]

Secession and war ended Lincoln's hopes of simultaneously resolving the slavery problem and saving the Union. His primary concern now became the restoration of unity to the broken nation, and the Negro was only a pawn in that struggle. So in both Emancipation Proclamations he left slavery intact in those border states that had remained loyal to the Union. It was not that he did not regard slavery as an evil, but like many Americans of his day he regarded the destruction of the Union as a greater evil. Jaffa, who is charitable toward Lincoln in searching for evidence of his real opposition to slavery, still says, "In a sense, it is true that Lincoln never intended to emancipate the Negro: what he intended was to emancipate the American republic from the curse of slavery, a curse which lay upon both races, and which in different ways enslaved them both.[16]

Thus, Negroes gained both freedom and citizenship as a result of a war in which neither was originally a paramount goal. The radical abolitionists viewed the conflict from the outset as a war to free the slaves, but the draft riots in the North and the reluctance with which the Union government finally agreed to arm Negro soldiers reflected the widespread feeling that this was a white man's war to save a white man's union!

· Frederick Douglass: Mirror of His Time

Nowhere can there be found better clues as to why the Negro failed to achieve full citizenship than in the experiences and observations of Frederick Douglass. Of all the self-made men who bear witness to the theme of opportunity in America, he is the greatest unsung hero. Booker T. Washington, a better-known symbol of Negro self-improvement, was born a slave as the Peculiar Institution was in its death throes; Douglass spent the first twenty years of his life as a captive of the institution when it was at its strongest. During the next fifty-eight years of his life, he rose from the perilous position of a fugitive slave to the honored status of Minister to Haiti. Self-educated, he became both a stirring orator and also a brilliant writer. Certainly he was not typical of the Negroes of his times, either slave or free. But he constantly tested the limits of the freedom and dignity that white Americans of all persuasions allowed Negroes. Because he was never willing to accept anything but full human dignity, his life was filled with a succession of high hopes and bitter disappointments.

One of his first disillusionments following his escape to the North came at the hands of his white abolitionist friends. Sent on a lecture tour through eastern Massachusetts, he learned the truth that it is easier for even the best-disposed white man to regard the Negro as a cause than as a man in his own right. He writes,"I was generally introduced as a 'chattel'—a 'thing'—a piece of southern property—the chairman assuring the audience that *it* could speak." [17] Reading and thinking for himself, he wanted to speak his own piece, but his abolitionist friends insisted, "Give us the facts: we will take care of the philosophy." [18] Douglass could not bring himself to heed their injunction for long; he became increasingly independent. When he eventually became his own man with his own philosophy of abolitionism, which conflicted with Garrison's, the split with his first friends in the North was filled with personal acrimony. His last disagreement with Garrison, on the question of the disbanding of the American Anti-Slavery Society in 1865, still reflected the tendency of the white abolitionists to regard the slave as a cause. Douglass wrote, "I felt that the work of the society was not done and that it had not fulfilled its mission, which was not merely to emancipate, but to elevate the enslaved class. But against Mr. Garrison's leadership, and the surprise and joy occasioned by the emancipation, it was impossible to keep the association alive. . . ." [19]

In Douglass' writings about his years as an abolitionist leader in the North, he castigated northern white people no less for their color prejudice and their obedience to the fugitive slave laws than southerners for their practice and defense of slavery. And, sometimes sadly, sometimes bitterly, he criticized his white friends and supporters for their failure to see the dimensions of the task that had to be performed to make the Negro a full-fledged member of American society. With emancipation accomplished, many of the strongest antislavery men saw their work as finished. Of the period before the adoption of the Fifteenth Amendment, Douglass wrote:

> The demand for the ballot was such a vast advance upon the former objects proclaimed by the friends of the colored race, that it startled and struck men as preposterous and wholly inadmissible. Anti-slavery men themselves were not united as to the wisdom of such a demand. Mr. Garrison himself, though foremost for the abolition of slavery, was not quite ready to join this advanced movement.[20]

When the Radical Republicans gained control of Congress, Douglass saw a period of great hope that his ambitions for the Negro might be fulfilled. The Fourteenth and Fifteenth Amendments were added to the Thirteenth, and civil rights laws were passed. Unfortunately, not even these accomplishments indicated a genuine concern for the future of the Negro people in America. In his biography of Douglass, Benjamin Quarles observes:

> Douglass believed that participation in political life was the normal condition of man. On the other hand, the Radicals (aside from Sumner) were completely indifferent to the Negro's political capacity. They looked upon Negro suffrage as a means of punishing the South and as a guaranty that the control of the national government would remain in Republican hands.[21]

Even as Douglass' hopes soared, he saw the beginning of the process that led to his bitterest disillusionment. As the southern states began to return to the Union, he saw the Republican party begin to appease the white delegates from these and the border states, and he saw white people of the North softening their attitudes toward their errant white brethren of the South even as they tired of the Negro problem. In 1883, he gave voice to the depths of his despair when, in an eight-to-one decision, the Supreme Court declared the Civil Rights Law of 1875 unconstitutional; at the same time, his voice was one of accurate prophecy. Of this decision, he wrote:

> In further illustration of the reactionary tendencies of public opinion against the black man, and of the increasing decline, since the war for the Union, in the power of resistance to the onward march of the rebel states to their former control and ascendency in the councils of the Nation, the decision of the United States Supreme Court, declaring the Civil Rights Law of 1875 unconstitutional, is striking and convincing. The strength and activities of the malign elements of the country against equal rights and equality before the law seem to increase in proportion to the increasing distance between that time and the time of the war. . . . From the hour that the loyal North began to fraternize with the disloyal and slaveholding South, from the hour that they began to "shake hands over the bloody chasm," from that hour the cause of justice to the black man began to decline and lose its hold upon the public mind, and it has lost ground ever since.[22]

Throughout his life, Douglass perceived with terrible clarity the fact that the liberty and dignity of the Negro could never be secure so long as it depended on the benevolence of white men rather than on the power of the Negro himself. After the war and emancipation, he declared:

> Though slavery was abolished, the wrongs of my people were not ended. Though they were not slaves, they were not yet quite free. No man can be truly free whose liberty is dependent upon the thought, feeling, and actions of others, and

who has himself no means in his own hands for guarding, protecting, defending, and maintaining that liberty. . . . The law on the side of freedom is of great advantage only where there is power to make that law respected. I know no class of my fellow-men, however just, enlightened, and humane, which can be wisely and safely trusted absolutely with the liberties of any other class.[23]

· The Decline of Negro Power

Douglass saw in the enfranchisement of the Negro the greatest hope for the achievement of real equality. Concentrated in the former states of the Confederacy, bewildered, and politically inexperienced, Negroes were unable to take significant advantage of the power of the ballot before it began to slip away from them. The effective disfranchisement of Negro voters in the South toward the turn of the century made possible the restoration of white, Protestant, rural dominance. In the North, the shift from rural dominance was beginning; but it was white, European immigrants who provided the basic ingredients for the new urban political power. In the West, even Orientals and Mexicans found that they did not fit the standard of Anglo-conformity on which the emerging sense of peoplehood in a nation of immigrants was based. As the United States became a world power with foreign territories inhabited by dark-skinned natives, the nation took up the "white man's burden" and with it the attitude of condescension and paternalism. Beginning with the administration of President Taft, the White House became increasingly white in spirit as well as in appearance. Both federal employment and the city of Washington became more and more segregated. Rural southern influence in the United States Senate, in House committees, and in the councils of the Democratic party made the plight of the Negro a political issue on which no aspiring white politician wanted to risk his political fortunes.

While northern politicians might denounce lynchings and the poll tax, there was not enough real concern over the condition of the Negro in the South to overcome the power of the filibuster. In the twenties, not even the Communists with nothing to lose politically by forthright stands on unpopular causes understood the aspirations of the Negroes or had any real sympathy for them. In 1927, they advanced as their solution to the American race problem the creation of a Negro republic in the South, modeled on the pseudo-autonomous ethnic republics of the Soviet Union.[24]

· The New Deal and the Negro

Not until the great crusade of the New Deal did the condition of Negroes in the United States begin to change materially as a result of the workings of the political process. Then the benefits came indirectly, not because greater rights for Negroes were a primary goal of the crusade. Negroes shared in the benefits of the New Deal primarily because they were among the great mass of underprivileged Americans whom Franklin D. Roosevelt welded into a powerful political majority dedicated to the principal that a minimum standard of welfare should be guaranteed to every American. By 1932, there were enough Negro voters in key precincts in northern cities to make them valuable allies. Even then, the payoff to Negroes for their support of Roosevelt was not always made with sound coin.

Negroes did benefit economically from relief programs, social security, old age pensions, public housing projects, and to a limited extent from minimum wage laws. The Negro upper class shared in the general prosperity which gradually returned to the economy as a result of New Deal legislation and the advent of World War II. But the National Labor Relations Act helped the Negro only to the extent that he was able to find a foothold in traditionally white unions by other than political means; it contained no guarantees against racial discrimination by employers or unions. The Agricultural Adjustment Act destroyed the Negro's position as the foundation stone of southern agriculture. Most important, the Democratic victories from 1932 to 1948 strengthened the white Democratic political establishment in the southern states and in the Congress, for the Solid South was as important to the national party as was the Negro vote in the North.

Nevertheless, history has shown that the shift of Negro voters to the party of Roosevelt in 1936 was the beginning of Negro political power. By the beginning of World War II, the Democratic strategists had learned that the Negro masses in key precincts of northern states were an essential part of their coalition, and Republican strategists were beginning to recognize that they must recapture at least part of that vote to have a chance of survival. Yet the power of the southern block in Congress and in the Democratic party still far overwhelmed this new Negro power in matters of legislation. The day when southern senators could no longer mount a successful filibuster against a pro-Negro bill was still far away.

· World War II

World War II postponed the Negro's drive for a showdown over his status. Even though Negro workers suffered discrimination during the war, full employment in the economy forestalled the development of the widening economic gap between whites and Negroes that was to become apparent later. Except for efforts to end segregation and discrimination in the federal government itself, the attack on the principle of segregation, begun in 1917 in *Buchanan v. Worley* and continued in *Gaines v. Canada* in 1938, was muted for the duration.[25] The most significant sign of a growth of Negro power was the effectiveness of A. Philip Randolph's threat to lead a march on Washington. When Roosevelt issued the executive order against discrimination in federal employment he confirmed the fact that Negroes could exercise a veto power in national affairs and that they could bargain effectively with this negative power.

At the end of World War II, the Old Regime seemed healthy enough. Although God was not necessarily a white Protestant American, few church leaders seemed to doubt that He would be perfectly comfortable in a segregated church. After all, He could visit the Negroes in *their* church on the following Sunday and perhaps take a freewill offering from the white congregation for the support of their missionary work among Negroes. Rural white legislators still held preeminence in statehouses all over the country, and southern senators and congressmen still wielded the weapons of seniority and the filibuster. As Negroes fled from unemployment and segregation in the South, they found themselves in the black ghettoes of northern and western cities and in the lower echelons of industry. As the black ghettoes grew and burst their boundaries, white people could flee to the lily-white suburbs. Negroes still sent their children to *de facto* segregated and inferior schools. They worshipped in segregated churches. In the North, they could elect Negro councilmen, legislators, and congressmen from their segregated districts, but the most they could expect these representatives to do for them was to dispense patronage. It was still a white man's country.

· Cracks in the Old Regime

Yet signs of cracks in the foundation of the Old Regime were already present. An increasing number of white politicians were becoming sensitive both to the importance of the Negro vote and to foreign criticism of American racial practices. Both white and

Negro Americans still smarted from the impact of the contradiction between these practices and the recent war against German racism. The march on Washington movement of 1942 had demonstrated that because of this inconsistency Negroes could embarrass the nation to the point of getting executive action in spite of congressional reluctance.

Most important, the Legal Defense Fund of the National Association for the Advancement of Colored People had developed a nearly completed brief against the principle of separate but equal, plus a staff of lawyers with the skill and acumen to plead their case. In the Sipuel, Sweatt, and McLaurin cases during the first five years after the end of the war, they had persuaded the Supreme Court to narrow the definition of equality, so that there remained only the bare principle that segregation was constitutional only if there were real equality. Now the NAACP was ready to attack that principle.

III

The Quiet Beginning and the Forgotten Heroes

A revolution does not begin with a declaration of war and a frontal assault on the Old Regime. It begins with incidents that, although noteworthy, are not fully appreciated for their long-run significance. Often those who are the instruments for lighting the fuse of revolution have no conception of the variety and magnitude of the forces for change that they set in motion. Many of the complacent beneficiaries of the status quo fail to see the early incidents of a revolution as serious, although the adamant extremists are quick to sound the alarm. The full significance of the beginning of a revolution is usually seen only in retrospect, after the movement is well under way.

By the same token, the heroes of the earliest stages of a revolutionary movement often appear timid and moderate in retrospect. As new leaders arise and displace them, these early heroes and their works are forgotten or even deprecated.

· The Significance of "Black Monday"

Such an incident was the school desegregation decision of the United States Supreme Court, rendered on May 17, 1954. The forgotten heroes are the lawyers of the National Association for the

Advancement of Colored People, who worked so long to secure this ruling. Whether Thurgood Marshall and his associates would have quailed at the possibility of bloodshed ten years later in Birmingham, Selma, Philadelphia, Rochester, Harlem, and Los Angeles is doubtful. That they did not envision the carnage and pillage of the long hot summers of the sixties is certain. But if we seek to identify a specific beginning point for the Negro Revolution, it was the day labeled "Black Monday" by that ideologist of reaction Judge Tom Brady of Mississippi. Brady and other spiritual descendants of the fire-eating secessionists of 1860 perceived intuitively that the legal foundation of white supremacy had been destroyed when the separate but equal doctrine was abandoned. Their anguished response proved the wisdom of the folk adage, "hit dog hollers!"

More temperate white southerners, of whom there were many, deplored the decision but found consolation in the thought that, like prohibition, this would be another noble experiment doomed to failure. Outside the South, numerous practicing white supremacists did not even realize that their lives would be affected by the decision. Legally sustained segregation was a southern phenomenon they thought; its abolition would be a southern problem. It did not occur to white Americans outside the South, and perhaps not even to Negroes, that there was tinder in their cities which would eventually be ignited.

Nor did Negroes in the South comprehend that within a few years they would be battling in the streets, not in the courtroom. In research conducted among Negro leaders in communities throughout the state of Florida during the summer of 1954, an amazing optimism was found as to how smoothly and how quickly public schools would be desegregated. The majority thought that the transition would be effected within ten years or less! [1]

Louis Lomax describes the surge of hope and optimism among Negroes in these words:

It would be impossible for a white person to understand what happened within black breasts on that Monday. An ardent segregationist has called it "Black Monday!" He was so right, but for reasons other than the ones he advances: That was the day we won; the day we took the white man's laws and won our case before an all-white Supreme Court with a Negro lawyer, Thurgood Marshall, as our chief counsel. And we were proud.

But we were also naive.[2]

If this was a day of exorbitant hopes and pride for millions of Negro Americans, it was a day of well-earned triumph for Thurgood Marshall and the leaders of the NAACP. They had proved their right to claim the leadership of the millions of Negroes in the United States, even though the actual membership of the association included less than 2 percent of that number. Years of legal research, decades of frustration at the slow pace of judicial action, and hours of rehearsal at the Howard University Law School had all been justified in a moment of victory. Thurgood Marshall, even in the striped pants and cutaway coat he wore before the bench of the highest court, was the symbol of the latest version of the New Negro. The NAACP's days of glory were numbered, however. A perennial problem, the fact that it had never been a mass organization, continued to plague the association.

· The Discontented Elite

An old jibe aimed at the NAACP is that it should be called "The National Association for the Advancement of *Certain* Colored People." Throughout its history it has been, in terms of its membership, an association of the elite. It has been under constant challenge to prove its concern for the masses of Negroes. Yet it has always been a discontented elite, and such elites play a crucial part in revolutions.

A discontented elite concerns itself with the hardships and frustrations of the masses. It speaks for the masses when they cannot speak for themselves, formulating coherent programs of change out of the inchoate welter of specific grievances. But it is not of the masses, and its position of leadership is insecure. Despite its critical role in the whole Negro protest movement, the period during which the NAACP stood secure and unchallenged at the pinnacle of Negro leadership was a brief one. Until its victory in the school cases of 1954, it had to contend with the fear of many Negroes, particularly in the South, that it was so radical as to be dangerous. Since the sit-ins of 1960, it has had to defend itself against the charge of being too conservative and "legalistic."

The NAACP, an association strongly identified with northern Negro intellectuals, was founded partly as a response to the growing influence of Booker T. Washington and his Tuskegee movement. Washington's emphasis on industrial education and self-improvement and his accommodation to the fact of white power in the famous Atlanta Compromise speech enhanced his acceptability to whites and raised him to a position of paternalistic leadership among southern Negroes. It has been said of Washington:

> His spirit of compromise and conciliation is not in harmony with the spirit of protest of the 1960s, but at the time there was no realistic alternative to this type of leadership. Negroes had practically no resources or opportunities for protest and little support from any segment of the white population. Under the circumstances, vigorous protest activities would have been both futile and dangerous, perhaps suicidal.[3]

However true this may have been from the vantage point of Negroes in the South, and this is where most of them were in Washington's day, there was a small group of Negroes in the North who viewed compromise, not protest, as the dangerous course. At the same time certain white liberals saw in the race riots between 1900 and 1910 proof that Washington's tactics could not stem the resurgence of racism. From an alliance between these small bands of radicals sprang the NAACP. In announcing the goals of the organization, these forefathers of the Negro Revolution renounced the key points of the compromise that Washington had proposed for Negroes. They declared their goals to be equal education for Negroes, enfranchisement, and the abolition of enforced segregation. That these goals may have seemed remote and impractical to the masses of southern Negroes, and that their announcement brought down the wrath of the white power structure both North and South did not deter this discontented, visionary elite.

The elite quality of this little group of Negro protest leaders is symbolized by the background of their most famous and influential member, W. E. B. DuBois. Near the time of his death DuBois himself pointed to the contrast between himself and Washington:

> He and I came from different backgrounds. I was born free. Washington was born slave. He felt the lash of an overseer across his back. I was born in Massachusetts, he on a slave plantation in the South. My great-grandfather fought with the Colonial Army in New England in the American Revolution. I had a happy childhood and acceptance in the community. Washington's childhood was hard. I had many more advantages: Fisk University, Harvard, graduate years in Europe. Washington had little formal schooling.[4]

From the time of its founding the NAACP captured the allegiance, although not always the active support, of upper-class Negroes both in the North and in the South. But Washington's pragmatic philosophy of accommodation prevailed among the Negro masses and his style of compromising, paternalistic leadership became the model for the external behavior of numerous leaders in southern Negro communities until the fifties. Ralph Ellison in *The*

Invisible Man portrays a Negro college president who could have been Booker T. Washington but also could have been modeled after any of a score of other presidents who even today retain their chairs, although more in discomfort than in power. Whether he deserved it or not, it was Washington and not DuBois who inherited Frederick Douglass' mantle of Negro leadership. Indeed, as Gunnar Myrdal observed, "Washington was not only a national Negro leader, but actually held a virtual monopoly of national Negro leadership for several decades.[5]

It is not popular with militant Negroes and liberal whites to admit this today, for a common part of the ideology of a social movement is a revision of history to show that the aroused masses have never willingly yielded an inch to oppression. Yet the very structure of the Negro community in America today testifies to the widespread acceptance of the spirit of the Atlanta Compromise for half a century. Lomax, without referring to Washington, describes exactly how his doctrine has been carried out: "The Negro college, the Negro press, the Negro politician and the Negro church all have this flaw in common: they were born into a segregated world and set out to serve us with the view that our separate world would someday be equal. As a result, each of these, in a different way, has a stake in the *status quo*." [6]

· The Strategy of the Elite

In contrast to the uplifters who followed the guidelines of Washington, the NAACP represented from its inception an elite that was not only discontented but also dissident, refusing to accept the compromise even as a transitional tactic. Persistent in the face of day-to-day acceptance of segregation by the majority of Negroes, of the separatist solution proposed by Marcus Garvey in his Back-to-Africa movement, and of the revolution-*cum*-secession vision of the Communists, this organization kept alive the dream of full assimilation as the only acceptable goal for Negro Americans. But for all their determination and dedication, the strategists of the organization had to reckon with the realities of the situation, including their own limited membership, funds, and popular support. Over the years they were forced to husband their precious resources, employing them only in cases that promised to contribute to the over-all strategy of expanding the meaning of citizenship. They found it strategic to play a waiting game at times rather than risk defeat prematurely. "The NAACP has shrewdly attacked certain civil wrongs that appeared to be completely out of pace with changing political opinion. . . . The Association has always been reluctant to force the Supreme Court to decide, lest this be disastrous." [7] Critics have charged that the organization has been insensitive to the economic problems of the Negro masses, concentrating on rights that could be enjoyed only by DuBois' "Talented Tenth." Perhaps the selection of issues, such as the right to equal graduate and professional education for Negroes, did reflect the preoccupation of an upper-class elite with the problems of their peers, but it can also be explained in terms of strategy and limited resources. In 1944 Myrdal concluded:

> I have . . . come to the conclusion that the Association is working according to a quite clearly conceived tactical plan, which is only more far-seeing than is customary in America, particularly in the South. . . . It has selected its points of attack with care and has pushed the front with caution; sometimes it has preferred only to preserve a favorable defense position. . . .
>
> In this sense, the tactics of the NAACP are "opportunistic"—though within the framework of a long-range policy to reach full equality for Negroes. [8]

Whatever the reasons for adherence to this strategy, it is little wonder that many Negroes were unable to see the logic or the usefulness of the tactics employed. They were not manuevers designed to whip up mass enthusiasm or to increase the visibility of the organization. They were, rather, the tactics of a highly disciplined, intellectual cadre which could see the logic and necessity of a long-range strategy that took into account the many variables of the power situation. Its effect was, however, to give the NAACP the appearance of an elite pressure group, detached from the masses of Negroes.

Belatedly, the association did gain fame by its legal victories. In 1963, in a public opinion poll of a nationwide sample of Negroes, Louis Harris and Associates found that 45 percent of the Negroes interviewed mentioned the NAACP as the agency that had done the most for Negro rights.[9] It was cited more frequently than any other organization or individual, and was evaluated positively by 91 percent of the sample. As a result Harris and his coauthor William Brink stated, "The NAACP is *the* Negro mass organization in both the North and the South." [10] At the same time, Martin Luther King, Jr., picked by 26 percent of the sample and evaluated positively by 88 percent, ranked higher than any other *individual* Negro, including NAACP President Roy Wilkins and legal counsel Thurgood Marshall. This too is significant.

Brink and Harris conclude, "There is no doubt that Dr. King comes closer to being the single mass leader of the Negro Revolution than any other man today." [11]

· Leadership: The New Style

Revolutions move not on the percentages of opinion polls, but on the feet of demonstrators. Leaders respond to the strident demands of the most insistent of their followers, not to the calmly expressed attitudes of a random sample no matter how much encouragement they may derive from the polls. Thus despite the recognition that

Brink and Harris found to be given the NAACP, the organization was already being overshadowed by Martin Luther King, Jr. It was King, the hero of the street battles, the cynosure of the headline writers, who represented the new style of Negro leadership. The NAACP had created the milieu in which his type could arise, but he had pre-empted the center of the stage.

In short, the NAACP, the discontented elite, started the revolution but it is doubtful that it will be the leader at the end. The belated blows of southern white politicians aimed at the NAACP following the 1954 decision came after the organization had achieved its most significant victory. It continued to win legal victories after 1954; but if the association had ceased to exist after that year, the Negro Revolution would still have erupted into the streets—perhaps even sooner than it did. The disillusionment of Negroes with the white man's law might have come sooner had the NAACP not still been winning victories of principle.

It is the long labor that went into the victory of 1954 that is being forgotten as the NAACP comes to be labeled a conservative organization. Thurgood Marshall, the hero of 1954, occupies a position of distinction and power as a justice of the Supreme Court, but he is far removed from the ranks of revolutionary leadership. The name of Charles Houston, his mentor, is little known even among Negroes, and the fame of Walter White is fading. Yet these men, along with Lloyd Gaines, Ada Lois Sipuel, G. W. McLaurin, and Oliver Brown, were the engineers and the pioneers who established the context in which the next generation of Negro leaders and heroes arose.

· The New Milieu

What was this milieu? How did it differ from the situation during the forties when signs of Negro discontent with the compromise of 1895–1896 were already rising?

First, it was a situation in which *hope* was added to discontent. Lerone Bennett, Jr., traces the relation between the two periods in these words, "The Big Change in Negro life occurred not in the sixties but in the forties. The only things wanting were a voice to give tongue to it, an instrument to contain it and a detonating spark. The detonating spark was the Supreme Court decision of 1954 which was the result of a long and brilliant legal campaign by the NAACP." [12]

The authority of the law of the land was now cast on the side of change, not on the side of the status quo. Any Negro with even the vaguest idea of what the Supreme Court had said now had good reason to hope for an improvement in his life and, even more so, in the life of his children.

More significantly, no Negro could any longer call himself a leader unless he challenged the validity and the necessity of segregation. The day of the compromise leader was over, even in the South, for the legal underpinnings of the compromise had been destroyed. Just as a white leader could no longer defend segregation without putting himself in defiance of the federal law, no Negro leader could accept it without betraying the hopes of his followers.

Still for a short time, there was no revolutionary fervor, no open and disrespectful challenge to the white man's law. The major part of the two years following May 17, 1954, was marked by legal maneuvering on both sides. Through suits directed not only against segregated schools but at other public accommodations the NAACP sought to extend the principle of the Brown decision, and it did so with marked success. Simultaneously, southern white politicians indicated their intention to defy or circumvent the new legal principle and they prepared appropriate tactics. The naïveté of any Negro who believed that the white community would willingly change its ways even with "deliberate speed" became evident. When the public schools of the South opened in September, 1955, four months after the Supreme Court had called for compliance with all deliberate speed, it was obvious that the phrase "the law of the land" had a hollow ring to it.

· The "Higher Law"

But the principle of the Brown decision did not long remain just the law of the land, just another interpretation of the Constitution by nine old men. It was rapidly transmuted into a "higher law." In discussing the role of law as educator, Jack Greenberg, of the NAACP, declares, "*Brown v. Board of Education* and its progeny changed more hearts and minds than all the sermons preached between 1954 and the present. Indeed, it changed a good many sermons." [13]

Greenberg's afterthought inadvertently suggests a reevaluation of the much deprecated role of religion in the Negro Revolution. It may be postulated that the activities of the major religious denominations during the months following the Brown decision corresponded roughly to that element that has been identified as "the desertion of the intellectuals." [14] The thinkers and the talkers of a society on the verge of revolution, however ineffective they may seem, shape the ideology of the revolutionary movement.

There is no need to lament again the failure of the white churches to take the lead in denouncing the evil of segregation before the Supreme Court did so. Nor is there need to review the failure of the churches as institutions to put their own houses in order, particularly at the parochial level. Campbell and Pettigrew have dramatically described the discrepancy between the resolutions passed at the national and regional level by the major denominations and the irresolution of parish ministers in the face of the social religion of their flocks.[15] But the function of the resolutions themselves should not be overlooked, for some people were listening to them—people who in a few years would be defying the power of the secular authorities in demonstrations. Although the white churches proved to be poor vehicles for the protest activities of their members, their official pronouncements encouraged many individual Christians to enter the fray.

The civil rights movement has had (and is having) a tremendous impact on organized religion in America, but the interaction has not been all one way. Father Joseph Fichter says of the interaction of religion and the movement, "What has come to the fore in the Civil Rights Movement is the prophetic, creative, and positive role of religion, which has long been recognized almost exclusively in the area of personal piety and family morality." [16]

Of course the prophetic voice heard from the churches after they began to repent following the 1954 court decision has not evoked the same response in all who heard it. As has always been true of the voice of prophecy, many who heard it were temporarily troubled in conscience, but like the rich young man of the Bible, "went away sorrowful because they had great possessions," possessions secured by the old order. As Campbell and Pettigrew have shown, this included ministers as well as laymen. Others shouted back with their own racist dogma, defending segregation as the way of God and denouncing the religious leaders of Protestantism and even Catholic bishops as false prophets. But what was the message heard by those who attended to the voice of the church?

It was very simply summed up in the statement of a Negro woman in Montgomery when she heard that the United States Supreme Court had ruled against segregated bus seating: "God has spoke from Washington, D.C." [17] In somewhat more sophisticated terms the National Council of the Churches of Christ said the same thing when, on May 19, 1954, its General Board declared, "The unanimous decision of the Supreme Court that segregation in the public schools is unconstitutional gives a clear status in law to a fundamental Christian and American principle." [18] Thus belatedly, after a court of men had spoken, the churches remembered that they were supposed to be responsive to a law higher than that of man.

Although the Supreme Court must obviously have been in error as long as it left unchanged the separate but equal principle, and, though its human fallibility was manifest in the fact that it had reversed itself, this new doctrine was not to be seen just as the law of the land; it was acclaimed as the law of God. Fichter, looking at this juncture of the legal and the political realms, says:

> The great practical impact on the moral pronouncements of religious leaders about racial integration stems in part from the fact that they are so completely in accord with the democratic values of the American culture. Religious and political motivations are mutually supportive—the politician can use scripture to confirm constitutional arguments, and the religious spokesman can use the principles of democracy to confirm the need for brotherhood under God.[19]

If American democratic values were so unambiguous and internally consistent, if the rulings of the many courts of the nation comprised only affirmations of broad principles such as liberty and equality, the relationship between the religious and the political realms would be as simple and as mutually supportive as Fichter implies. But freedom and equality involve ultimate contradictions, and courts must struggle with the application of general principles to specific cases. The implementation decree issued by the Supreme Court in 1955, leaving discretionary powers in setting the pace of school desegregation in the hands of lower courts, was obviously the voice of human judges balancing the conflicting rights and interests of different classes of citizens. It was not the voice of God thundering "Thou shalt not. . . ." Subsequent events would show

that the desegregation orders of the courts would not be as unequivocal and compelling as the mandate felt in the hearts of those
Americans who accepted the principle of desegregation as higher
law. As Crane Brinton observed of the English, American, and
French revolutions, "That nature always counseled what the
intellectuals in revolt wanted is an observation we must in these
days feel bound to make." [20]

· The Social Scientists

The intellectuals of organized religion justified integration as a
value in terms of Judeo-Christian and democratic principles—the
principles underlying the American creed, according to Myrdal.
But the churchmen spoke to a society in which natural law is more
likely to be viewed as a product of scientific investigation than of
divine revelation. Hence another group of intellectuals, already
isolated from the common man by their constant debunking of his
popular theories of human nature, played a part in the desertion of
the intellectuals. These were the social scientists. Although the
church leaders hailed the Supreme Court decision as confirming
the law of God, the Court itself turned to the findings of science to
justify its reasoning! In turn, the scientists found themselves in the
position not only of justifying the conclusions of their researches,
but also of defending the legal and moral principles now explicitly
derived from these theories.

Because of their professional judgment that the theories were
valid, and because of the egalitarian and humanitarian ethos of the
social sciences, many sociologists, psychologists, and anthropolo-
gists played the dual role of scientist and ideologist with force and
conviction. Without gainsaying the validity of the conclusion that
segregation is psychologically harmful to its victims, it must be
recognized that the typically skeptical, even querulous, attitude of

scientists toward each other's work was largely suspended in this case.

In the mid-fifties it was not enough for the social scientist to affirm his belief that the question of the harmful effects of segregation was now closed in order to escape suspicion of being either senile, bigoted, or mercenary. Even to examine the difficulties of achieving the goals of desegregation and assimilation with any but an optimistic bias was suspect. The proposition that a firm and unequivocal posture on the part of public authorities could overcome resistance to desegregation became almost an article of faith. That most of these same public authorities were guardians of the interests of the Old Regime was largely overlooked. So also was the fact it was not just the prejudiced attitudes of individual white people but the whole social structure that sustained segregation. The statement by Milton Gordon about intergroup relations work applies almost as well to research on desegregation. "I exaggerate only slightly when I state that, *in terms of the crucial considerations of social structure*, intergroup relations work in the United States proceeds like a race horse galloping along with blinders." [21]

If Negroes were naïve in expecting that white Americans would follow the law of the land, they were certainly encouraged in this belief by the optimism of social scientists and by the repentance of the churches. College campuses and those local churches in which the clergy dared to speak out became the symbols of the desertion of the intellectuals from the Old Regime. Among white people, liberal professors, students, and preachers were among the first targets of the emerging resistance movement. In some instances Negroes placed undue faith in both the numbers and influence of these white liberals and thus made deeper the disillusionment that was yet to come.

· The Rise of a Prophet

While the ideology of the Negro protest movement was undergoing
rapid development following May 17, 1954, the movement still
lacked any program other than the legal tactics of the NAACP.
Worse yet, it lacked a prophet. Martin Luther King, Jr., provided
both.

The first eighteen months after the Brown decision was an interlude of philosophizing, mobilizing—and waiting. As has been
shown, the intellectuals were busy explaining to all who would lis-
ten that the decision was both right and practical. Nevertheless, a
resistance was mobilizing in the South, dedicated to the proposition that desegregation was not inevitable. Except for the NAACP
lawyers and their clients, Negroes were waiting to see how the
South would react to the new law. So also was the President of the
United States.

Then, on December 1, 1955, Mrs. Rosa Parks acted as if the new
legal principle would make a difference; she refused to be moved
from her bus seat. There followed what Louis Lomax calls "the
Birth of the Revolt"—the Montgomery bus boycott. In the light of
the events of the next ten years, this confrontation seems mild and
peaceful; but out of it emerged certain factors that would be of
enduring importance in the movement. The first was the new type
of leadership personified by Martin Luther King, Jr. The second
was the fact that this type of protest leadership emerged in the
midst of mass action by Negroes. Unlike the old accommodating
leaders, even unlike the militant but elite leadership of the earlier
NAACP, the new Negro leader could no longer retain his position
by doing things *for* his people; he had to do things *with* them. He
had to march!

The third factor, intricately related to the personal leadership of

King but far-reaching in its effects, was the philosophy of nonviolent civil disobedience. On one level, nonviolent direct action can be viewed as merely a tactic that is extremely useful to a people faced with overwhelming power. There is no question that it was effective for a time in the struggle; the limits of what it could accomplish have yet to be ascertained.

On another level nonviolence can be viewed as a philosophy of interpersonal relations—the view that King himself seems to prefer. Rooted in the teachings of Jesus, of Thoreau, of Gandhi, it can be reduced to concise homilies such as "overcome evil with good," and "love thine enemy." Lomax observed of King, "He is the first Negro minister I have ever heard who can reduce the Negro problem to a spiritual matter and yet inspire the people to seek a solution on this side of the Jordan, not in the life beyond death." [22] In exactly this sense King became the prophet of the revolution. He reduced the complex problem of the segregated, unequal social structure to a simple spiritual equation: segregation is evil, integration is good. At the same time, he showed his followers concrete ways to attack the visible, accessible symbols of evil. This attack, nonviolent though it was, had all the attraction of aggression for Negroes who had for so long concealed their hostility from whites. Here at last was an honest confrontation in which the Negro, clothed in robes of nonviolent righteousness, forced the white sinner to give up his sinful ways or to practice them in the eyes of the world.

· Nonviolence as a Revolutionary Strategy

The nonviolence practiced by Negro Americans and their white allies in the face of incredible provocation has been one of the miracles of modern United States history. Adherence to the form, if not always to the philosophy, of nonviolence for a while preserved an image of the Negro protest movement as respectable, Christian, and nonrevolutionary. But emphasis on nonviolence as a tactic and as a philosophy has obscured the fact that nonviolent direct action can also be a revolutionary strategy. Gandhi did not just bring reforms in the British administration of India; he threw the British out by passive resistance. The general strike, another form of nonviolent resistance, may be simply a tactic in a continuing dialogue between management and labor over terms of employment. It may also be a weapon for overthrowing a government, and has long been advocated as such by avowed revolutionists. This is not to suggest that the young Martin Luther King thought of starting a revolution when he became the spokesman of nonviolent direct action in Montgomery. He did, however, offer Negroes a tactic that could become the basis for a revolutionary strategy, and a philosophy that would be hard to maintain as the battle grew fiercer.

The intellectuals of the major religious denominations had appealed to the rank and file of their churches to comply with the desegregation rulings of the Supreme Court because they reflected not only the law of the land but also the law of God. But King did not speak of mere compliance; his followers had been complying with segregation laws for too long already. Although the principle of separate but equal had been overthrown, many specific laws sustaining the system of segregation remained untested. The new prophet spoke, therefore, of resistance, of noncooperation with evil, of civil disobedience.

· Civil Disobedience

Yet civil disobedience was not first introduced into the struggle by the advocates of integration, as much as it has been associated with their cause. It should never be forgotten that southern white segre-

gationists, in the face of the Court's decision, shouted "never!";
that southern legislatures passed resolutions of interposition; that
southern white political candidates offered to serve their terms in
jail rather than obey the federal courts; and that a southern
governor attempted to use the National Guard to enforce segregation in defiance of a court order to desegregate. This act of
Governor Faubus backfired for the resistance movement, of
course. The crisis of Little Rock showed that if Negroes persisted
in claiming their new rights and the resistance persisted in denying
them, a local crisis could become a national one requiring even an
apathetic, aloof federal executive to become involved.

Thus by 1957 the fundamental premises had been laid down for
a significant shift in the strategy of the Negro protest movement
away from the historic reliance of the NAACP on the normal legal
and political processes. The first premise was inherent in the philosophy of King, the new prophet: that since segregation laws were
evil, to disobey them was not only justified but required by the
higher law. The second basis emerged from the experience of Little
Rock: that by the creation of a crisis, social change could be
effected in spite of popular opposition and official apathy. Yet it
was not until nearly three years later that the shift in strategy
came. What had happened in the interim?

· The Revolutionary Cramp

In the early sixties two novel and seemingly contradictory developments in the Negro protest became headline news. One was the
onset of dramatically integrationist sit-ins and freedom rides. The
other was the emergence of militantly pluralistic, even secessionist,
activity by the members of the Nation of Islam, the "Black Muslims." Neither was entirely new, but there was a crescendo in the
volume of both at this time. Both, it may be argued, reflected the

full development of what has been called in revolutionary theory, "revolutionary cramp."

This term was introduced by George S. Pettee to describe a subjective sense of repression that is at the same time felt to be unnecessary. He said, "The cramped individual is one who not only finds that his basic impulses are interfered with, or that he is threatened by various ills, this is to say, who is deprived of liberty and security, but who also feels that this repression is unnecessary and avoidable, and therefore unjustified." [23]

Pettee used this concept of cramp to designate a phenomenon that, although familiar to students of revolution, never ceases to mystify contemporary defenders of the Old Regime. This is the fact that "a rising class, which is actually becoming constantly better off objectively, generally rebels most readily, and why the most severe repression has so often failed to cause a revolution." [24] Translated into the idiom of the times, many white Americans felt indignant that the Negro revolt should escalate at a time when "Negroes had never had it so good," when they had already made gains that seemed revolutionary to the segregationist.

It was these very gains that generated the types of cramp—ideological, social, economic, and political—that Pettee postulates as necessary conditions for revolution. It is the ideological cramp, the discrepancy between the promise of desegregation and the reality of tokenism, that has been most thoroughly analyzed as a cause of the outburst of direct action led largely by Negro college students. What constitutes social cramp had been even longer in developing. This was the growth both in size and in purchasing power of a Negro middle class. In spite of discrimination, in spite of the continued existence of a gap between the education, income, and occupation of whites and Negroes, both the number and the proportion of Negroes who might be termed middle class increased between 1940 and 1960. As much as the black bourgeoisie may be criticized for their retreat into a world of make-believe, they still remain whitewardly mobile. As their incomes increased and their tastes grew richer, they found many doors open to them as consumers. But even after the legal supports for segregation began to crumble, and even when they were able to pay their way, they found the same old social barriers standing firm. The segregated eating places in department stores constituted a perfect symbol of the cramp, the inconsistency, that these people felt. They were accepted, sometimes even welcomed, at all counters but one, for their purchasing power was significant. And to add yet another note of bitter irony, the one department in which they were not welcomed as customers was usually the only one at which members of their race might be employed, if only as dishwashers.

But the fight of the relatively well-off Negro for the right to spend his money where he pleased temporarily obscured the fact that at the other end of the scale a growing proportion of Negroes had virtually no money to spend. Here was the economic cramp, reflected in the growing bitterness and frustration of unskilled, undereducated Negroes who found jobs that they could fill growing scarcer as the society became more affluent. Their disillusionment with a white America in which there seemed to be no place for them was voiced first by the most radical spokesmen of the revolution—the Muslims and the angry writers like James Baldwin. The new leaders, such as Martin Luther King, Jr., were still concentrating their attacks on segregation, the symbol of inequality, but not the painful physical reality. In February, 1965, Bayard Rustin, a close associate of King and organizer of the 1963 March on Washington, admitted, "We must recognize that in desegregating public accommodations, we affected institutions which are relatively peripheral both to the American socio-economic order and to the fundamental conditions of life of the Negro people." [25]

Even so, as late as Spring, 1964, leaders such as King and Rustin were insisting that the public accommodations section of the civil rights act was the crucial portion of the proposed legislation, the portion without which the bill would become a farce. Yet that same summer was marked by the first outburst of riots in northern cities where poverty and its sequelae, not the symbolism of segregation, were clearly the issue.

Ideological, social, and economic cramp all intensified during the decade following the desegregation decision of 1954. But the sort of cramp that is of most interest here, because it has contributed most to the circumstances that make the Negro protest movement truly a revolution, is what Pettee calls political cramp. This, simply expressed, is the inability of the machinery of government to adjust quickly and decisively enough to satisfy the demands of the discontented classes. The stability that a constitution provides becomes a source of danger to the established government in a crisis. Pettee observes:

> Procedural difficulties in the amending process are the critical point in all cramp due to the constitution of the government itself. . . . In the efforts of a discriminating fraction of the elite to follow an intelligent conservative policy in the midst of die-hards and radicals, the difficulty of legal amendment may prove to be the straw that breaks the camel's back. The lack of a general perception of this in America is probably the clearest and most dangerous of all the weaknesses in the situation. The dice are loaded heavily against anything but outright revolution or die-hard reaction. . . .[26]

Although he wrote in the context of the crisis of the Great Depression, not of the civil rights crisis, Pettee's observations are still highly pertinent. As was pointed out in Chapter I, the intricate system of checks and balances that characterizes the American system of government constitutes a powerful bulwark against rapid and boldly planned change. For this reason, gradualism in the implementation of the principle of the school desegregation decision and its corollaries was inevitable. In spite of the attention that they have attracted by the viciousness of their tactics, it is not the extremists of the resistance movement who have been most influential in retarding the pace of social change. The gradualism and tokenism that became so frustrating to Negroes were created primarily by legalists who did not crudely defy the law but cleverly used it to limit change to a minimum. Indeed, it seems almost as if the extremists of the resistance movement have been inadvertent allies of Negroes because their proclivity for creating crises brought the stigma of lawlessness on the whole resistance movement and accelerated change by inviting federal intervention!

James Vander Zanden characterizes the position of the effective, moderate, southern leaders vis-à-vis their constituents in these words, "We have done everything possible to prevent desegregation. We can do no more. We are now confronted with a situation where we will have to accept some Negroes from time to time in a number of our white schools. But we will do all in our power to make certain that such Negroes will be held to a minimum. We will maintain our southern way of life." [27]

As legal as this posture may have been, it still constituted a policy of gradualism, of limited change, of balancing what Negroes believed to be their rights against what white southerners (and many others, too) cherished as *their* rights. Negro leaders and their followers were caught up, however, in the grip of a mood of impatience that was incompatible with such a sedate pace of change. A revolutionary myth, a utopian vision, had developed to epitomize this mood.[28] The revolutionary myth was captured in the magic words, "Freedom Now." It was presaged by the theme adopted by the NAACP in 1957, "Free by Sixty-Three!" Its urgency and its breadth was underlined by Martin Luther King, Jr., in his famous statement, "The Negro wants all of his rights, he wants them here, and he wants them now!"

By the time this revolutionary myth and the spirit that accompanied it had developed, it was quite obvious that local and state governments in the South, and in some cases outside the South, would not willingly give the Negro all of his rights now or in the near future. It should also have been obvious that the federal government did not possess the power to grant freedom now, no matter how much sympathy for the plight of the Negro might be found among individual officials. Yet the slogan, "Freedom Now," and the strategy of using civil disobedience to force local governments into conflict with the federal authority implied such a demand on the national government. In the imperative tone of the appeals to the federal government to force state and local compliance lay the seeds of defiance of the federal government. If the day came when it did not accede to the demands of civil rights leaders, what then?

As late as 1963 this day had not come and, except in the South, it might be said that the Negro protest movement was not quite yet viewed as revolutionary. Accepting the Brink-Harris survey as an indication, there was extensive sympathy for the Negro's goals and still a slim margin of approval for demonstrations in general. There was strong disapproval of such tactics as sit-ins, picketing, and lie-ins.[29] People were beginning to feel that Negroes were pressing too hard and asking too much. Lie-ins at construction sites in northern cities had aroused a large measure of concern about Negro tactics; attacks on *de facto* segregation in some northern schools had awakened some northern whites to the fact that the civil rights crisis was not confined to the South. In truth, however, between 1954 and 1963 the South *was* the place where the action was. The major crisis centered around southern segregation, and it was the segregationist resistance that bore the stigma of lawlessness. Negroes were clearly in revolt, but the revolt was in the provinces, aimed at anachronistic state laws and recalcitrant southern officials who refused to accept the law of the land. It was not aimed at the federal government. That segregation no longer enjoyed the blessing of the Constitution was quite clear. The leaders of the Negro protest movement and the officials of the federal executive and judicial branches still seemed to be partners in the task of making equality a reality in southern communities.

IV

The Strategy of Protest

Like many other revolutions, the Negro Revolution began with skirmishes in the provinces (in this case the South) accompanied by protestations of unqualified loyalty to the central government. Moreover, when the attack on segregation by law in the South began, it appeared that this was to be the major battle in the war for equality. A decade later it became evident that this battle was only a preliminary to the larger conflict as the revolution became national, not provincial. What was forged in this first phase of the conflict was not a victory, but a strategy. The strategy developed in fighting the southern resistance would come to be used against a very different sort of resistance. This strategy would mold the public definition of the movement, bringing it closer and closer to the point of being defined as dangerous or revolutionary. In the process, the goals of the movement would undergo a metamorphosis, becoming broader yet vaguer.

· Initial Optimism Versus Southern Resistance

In retrospect, the optimism of Negroes in the years immediately after 1954 appears excessive. Yet this optimism is understandable in the light of the assumptions that underlay it.

The first assumption was that the real issue was segregation; it was the key that would unlock the door to equality. Thus in 1957, the NAACP proclaimed as its paramount goal, "the elimination of all state-imposed segregation by 1963." Emphasis on state-imposed segregation defined the battle as essentially a southern conflict. It failed to anticipate that by the fateful year of 1963 *de facto* segregation outside the South would be as crucial an issue as state-imposed segregation within the South. The myopic concentration of civil rights leaders on segregation during this period is analogous to the concentration of white abolitionists on slavery as an institution. In both cases there was a reluctance to look beyond the destruction of the institution to the rehabilitation of its victims.

Optimism was reflected even more clearly in the initial concentration on school desegregation. The optimism with which the school desegregation decision was regarded suggests that a domino theory of integration was tacitly accepted. The association of children in school would lead not only to better educated Negroes but also to less prejudiced whites, setting in motion a benign spiral of integration in all areas of life.

The assumption that state-imposed segregation was the key issue led easily to the second assumption that the white South was the enemy and that white people outside the South were potential allies. After all, the nonsouthern states had not taken advantage of the license granted in *Plessy v. Ferguson* to create a legal color line. Kansas and Delaware, the nonsouthern states involved in *Brown v. Board of Education*, had complied with the desegregation decision even before the Supreme Court held hearings on the implementation of the ruling. Now that the highest federal court had redefined the national morality, it was up to the wayward region with its historic attachment to the peculiar institution to rejoin the rest of the nation.

The third assumption was that even white southerners would be converted relatively easily; that they would be responsive to the rule of law and to the moral demands of the American creed. The theory still persists that had the Supreme Court stated the demands of the law unequivocally southern resistance would have been minimized. The ambiguous phrase, "with all deliberate speed," has been criticized as an invitation to resistance and delay. This theory minimizes the depth of southern white prejudice and ignores the nature of the judicial process.

It is true that the White Citizens Councils were formed during the year of grace following the 1954 decision and sprang into action immediately following the May 31, 1955 implementation decree. That it took a year for the resistance to reveal its strength does not mean that the white South was willing to accept desegregation. As James Vander Zanden has observed, during this first year "the mass of southern whites simply did not comprehend that desegregation could actually happen to them or to their communities." [1] An example of this attitude of disbelief was seen in Florida where Attorney General Richard Erwin decided to submit an *Amicus Curiae* brief in the hearings on the implementation decree. He was bitterly attacked from many quarters for surrendering to an unconstitutional court decision. One prominent lawyer argued that the state of Florida should not submit a brief because the problem belonged to the states of South Carolina and Virginia, and Florida should not get involved. Erwin's critics felt that he should have taken the position of another southern attorney general who proclaimed, "I will not help the Supreme Court select the knife with which to stab us in the back!"

Florida did, of course, become involved but not because the attorney general submitted his brief. The state, like every other southern state, became involved as soon as the NAACP brought suit against a local school board on behalf of a Negro child. But the 1955 implementation decree may not have been as critical as is often supposed. Whatever the nature of the decree, it would have applied immediately only to Prince Edward County, Virginia, and Clarendon County, South Carolina. The burden would still have fallen on Negro children and their parents to sue for desegregation school district by school district. The same legal maze could have been created that later was actually erected "by a huge volume of new statutes of varying degrees of ingenuity and effrontery." [2] By November, 1962, 379 such laws or resolutions had been passed in sixteen states.[3]

Even after it became evident that circumvention, not compliance, was to characterize the white South's reaction to the law, faith in the vulnerability of the southern white man's conscience persisted. Vincent Harding points out that in the Montgomery movement the promises held out to the aroused Negro masses were "promises of 'victory,' of 'winning' the enemy, of achieving desegregation, of creating 'the beloved community'." [4]

Because of the optimism based on these three assumptions, the Negro protest movement began with a strong emphasis on its values, presented as truly Christian and American. There was little emphasis on the theme of power. The relationship between power and the values of a movement is of great importance to the sort of public definition the movement gets.

· Power and Values in Social Movements

A social movement may emphasize the promotion of its values in society without explicit demands for the redistribution of power. Even if the emphasis is upon the values, movements may vary in the degree to which they rely upon persuasion rather than power to promote acceptance of these values. The more the movement resorts to power tactics, even as a temporary expedient, the more likely it is to develop a power-orientation, with the seizure of power becoming an end in itself. And as the power-orientation of a movement becomes stronger and more evident, it is more likely to be defined as dangerous or revolutionary by those classes in the society that already possess power and are threatened by any redistribution of it.

Movements rarely begin with an open avowal of a quest for power. They are most likely to do so when the leaders are already committed to an elitist philosophy, or when they anticipate such overwhelming opposition to their values that conflict and an overthrow of the Old Regime are deemed necessary. Neither of these conditions was present in the Negro protest movement in the fifties. The theme of black supremacy held by the Black Muslims was completely alien to the equalitarian philosophy of the NAACP and Martin Luther King, Jr. And as has been shown, the optimism of Negroes and their leaders suggested that right would make might. Power tactics should not be needed to make white Americans live up to the requirements of the Constitution. The white man's court had declared segregation illegal; the white churches were hastening to declare it sinful; why shouldn't the process of change be an orderly one, proceeding with all deliberate speed? And why should the advocates of desegregation, with both the law of man and the law of God on their side, need to resort to illegitimate means in order to assert their rights? Such tactics were needed only by the lunatic fringe of die-hard segregationists. *They* were the rebels, the defiers of law and order; they had launched a counterrevolution when there was no revolution, only a change in the law!

· **Revolution and Counterrevolution in the South**

But to white southerners, except for the deviant liberals of the region, there *was* a revolution. A counterrevolution was regarded as necessary if the southern way of life were to be preserved. There was a common tendency to equate lawfulness and orderly change with do-nothing gradualism; any effective action to promote change was defined as radical. This was symbolized by the common practice of contrasting the White Citizens Council and the NAACP as occupying the two radical or extremist positions in the spectrum of opinion and action. That the NAACP was advocating compliance with constitutional law while the Councils shouted, "Never," was overlooked. Even to moderate segregationists the values that the NAACP sought to promote were as revolutionary and as reprehensible as were the tactics used by the Citizens Council to oppose them. White liberals in the South knew, however, that a revolutionary struggle was beginning. They soon learned from harsh reprisals that it was not how you advocated desegregation, but that you advocated it at all that classified you as a traitor. By the same token, the topic of respectable public debate in the South, particularly in the political arena, was how to prevent or minimize desegregation.

It is ironic that the white South was extremely successful in minimizing the impact of the desegregation decisions of the federal courts without arousing the indignation of the rest of the nation. As much as the White Citizens Councils and the Ku Klux Klan are invoked as symbols of the southern resistance, they and their extralegal tactics did not make this possible. Far more effective were the legal stratagems, evasions, and delays that led Negroes to realize that although they had won a new statement of principle they had not won the power to cause this principle to be implemented. Vander Zanden's assessment of the second phase of resistance (between the implementation decision and Little Rock) suggests:

> The state governmental machinery and resources were at the disposal of whites, who were in a position to use them if they so chose to maintain segregation. Washington, with its vast federal machinery and resources, was the only adversary that could successfully defeat the South in its resistance efforts. And Washington was neither prepared to take—nor was the nation, it seems, at that time prepared to sanction—

such action, which, probably short of troops, could not compel compliance in the face of a solid, united South.[5]

The law, which had appeared to be at last on the side of the Negro, still proved to be a more effective weapon for minimizing desegregation than for promoting integration. And if the Negro protest movement were not defined as revolutionary outside the South, neither was the white resistance treated as revolutionary until the crisis at Little Rock.

Also ironic was the fact that both the desegregation of the buses in Montgomery and the desegregation of Central High School in Little Rock came ultimately through the exertion of legal power by the NAACP, not through the newer techniques of direct action. In Montgomery, the bus boycott demonstrated the potentialities for Negro mass protest and it promoted Martin Luther King, Jr., to his position as prophet of the movement. Victory over city hall and the bus company came, however, through a federal court decision won by the NAACP. In Little Rock, it was the persistence of the nine Negro students and their NAACP advisers in claiming the rights promised them by a federal court that forced President Eisenhower to use the full force of federal power against Governor Faubus.

At the same time, the victory in Little Rock marked a significant shift toward reliance on power rather than on persuasion. The soldiers standing in the halls of Central High School for weeks after the nine students were admitted symbolized this shift. Not the internal controls of respect for law or allegiance to the American creed, but the external control of the federal presence made desegregation work at Central High.

Thus Little Rock has been properly described as a turning point in the protest movement. In Vander Zanden's words, ". . . the intervention of federal troops served to demonstrate that the full resources of the federal government stood behind the courts in enforcing the desegregation rulings. That it would do so had not always been clear." [6] Yet it should be remembered that this new weapon, which overcame blatant southern defiance, still produced only token compliance. Little Rock marked but the beginning of a new phase of the resistance. Southern white lawyers and politicians still countered the legal maneuvers of the NAACP with prolonged litigation, pupil placement laws, tuition plans, and closed public facilities. School desegregation proceeded at a tortuously slow pace and the fabric of southern society remained segregated.

· **Disillusionment and the Strategy of Protest**

The Negro revolt of 1960 erupted as a new generation of Negroes seemed to sense that persuasion was not going to bring an end to segregation. They saw that the Negro minority was far more powerless than the earlier successes of the NAACP might suggest. Through its persistence and its shrewd assessment of both foreign relations and the mood of the court, the NAACP had secured a new judicial interpretation of the Fourteenth Amendment. In Little Rock, it had forced a reluctant federal executive to stand behind this new interpretation when in the eyes of the whole world Governor Faubus opposed it with state sovereignty. But now it was evident that Negroes did not possess the power, even with the support of the federal courts and the federal executive, to bring about more than token compliance. In the South, Negroes lacked the voting power to compel state and local officials to adopt an attitude of genuine compliance rather than one of reluctant tokenism. Negro votes counted heavily in some key northern states and in national elections. They did not represent enough power to dislodge the southern congressional bloc from its historic position as a barrier to any significant civil rights legislation. The civil rights struggle constituted the greatest domestic crisis since the Depression and an even greater threat to the United States' position as leader of the free world. Yet during the first decade of this crisis the legislative arm of the federal government passed no really strong civil rights laws. The acts that were passed dealt primarily and feebly with voting and left untouched the problems of segregation, employment, and housing.

Through resistance on the state level and a business-as-usual attitude on the national level, Negroes found the legitimate channels of effecting social change closed to them. To overcome this impasse they shifted to a strategy that relied on neither court action nor legislation—a strategy of protest through direct action. In terms of the new morality of desegregation the tactics of direct action were unquestionably moral. In some instances, as in the case of the freedom rides, they were legitimate, for the Supreme Court had long before removed the legal supports for segregation in transportation. But in some of the sit-ins, the mass marches, and the kneel-ins, the tactics were extralegal or even illegal. The law was either neutral, as in the case of the churches, or was against the demonstrators, as in cases when ordinances against trespass or disturbing the peace could be invoked by local authorities. The new appeal of the movement was not made to existing judicial rulings but to the higher law that had already been invoked by King and sanctioned by the major religious denominations. The tactic was nonviolent direct action deliberately risking both illegal and legal reprisals. The confrontations created by the use of the tactic were not merely test cases aimed at securing new definitions of rights. They were conflict situations created to force white power-wielders to bargain with Negroes. The history of the use of nonviolent direct action by the Congress of Racial Equality suggests that, in spite of all the talk of love by King and many other clergymen in the movement, the tactic is essentially part of a strategy of power, not persuasion.

Significantly, CORE did not originate in the pre-1954 South with its massive structure of segregation laws. It started in 1941 in

Chicago. The first sit-ins were used to force restaurateurs to comply with already existing public accommodations ordinances. The earliest freedom ride was taken by a CORE group in 1947 to ascertain whether bus companies operating in interstate transportation were complying with the ruling of the Supreme Court in *Morgan v. West Virginia.* It might be said that from its earliest days CORE displayed a profound mistrust of the willingness of white Americans to obey or enforce civil rights laws unless forced to do so.

The founders of CORE came from a background of Christian idealism and philosophic pacificism, and their model for action was nonviolence, or *Satyagraha,* as practiced by Gandhi and his followers in India. The nonviolence and altruism that are basic to *Satyagraha* should not be allowed to obscure the fact that in India and in South Africa it was a weapon of civil disobedience and of revolution. *Satyagraha* was adopted in situations in which legitimate, institutional means of seeking relief from injustice were deemed inadequate. And just such a situation was created in the South by a combination of civil disobedience and legalistic opposition. When the movement encountered this situation, the direct action organizations took the initiative away from the NAACP. The counterrevolution of the southern resistance had forced the Negro protest movement into the ways of revolution.

· A Power Strategy

The type of strategy that rests primarily on demonstrations, as the various forms of direct action have come to be called, has been analyzed under a variety of names. Richard Walton has called it a "power strategy," contrasting it with an "attitude change" strategy.[7] The former rests upon threats and coercion, the latter on "increasing the level of attraction and trust" between the parties involved in a changing social system. While the apostles of nonviolence have spoken a language of love and reconciliation, their actions have moved steadily in the direction of the naked display of power. There is an interesting inconsistency in Martin Luther King, Jr.'s argument against the forthright appeal of Robert F. Williams for the use of violent as well as nonviolent means of coercing justice from whites. King declared, "There is more power in socially organized masses on the march than there is in guns in the hands of a few desperate men. . . . Our powerful weapons are the voices, the feet, and the bodies of dedicated, united people, moving without rest toward a just goal." [8]

Here the philosophy of love and reconciliation has disappeared in the face of the strategy of power; the argument is essentially about types of power and their relative effectiveness. Also overlooked is the argument advanced by Walton and borne out by subsequent developments; "Where they are used, tactics of nonviolence are effective at least in part because the other group perceives this method as an alternative to violence. The option of violence is indirectly suggested by advocating nonviolence." [9]

James Q. Wilson has described this type of strategy as "a strategy of protest." He discusses protest as a form of bargaining, defined as "a situation in which two or more parties seek conflicting ends through the exchange of compensations. The essential element is that concessions are rewarded." [10]

The CORE formula for direct action reveals that protest demonstrations were indeed conceived as part of a bargaining process.[11] The general procedure recommended by national CORE to local protest groups specifies that an attempt to negotiate with the discriminating agent should be undertaken prior to the planning and implementation of a nonviolent protest demonstration. After the demonstration is launched, repeated attempts to negotiate differences should be made.

Although not all local groups (some were imitators of CORE, not branches of it), adhered to the suggestion to attempt negotiations before demonstrating, the relationship of demonstrations to negotiations soon came to be taken for granted by both parties. Thus the biracial committee was proposed by white moderates as a mechanism for bargaining. Despite the fact that such committees usually were denounced by militant Negroes as stalling devices, the demand for their creation became a standard item on the agenda of local protest movements.

Wilson's analysis of protest as a special form of bargaining suggests the reason why biracial committees have been so ineffective as forums for negotiation. He pointed out that protest is distinguished from bargaining "by the exclusive use of negative inducements (threats) that rely for their effect on sanctions which require *mass* actions or response." [12] The only compensation that Negro leaders could offer to white leaders in negotiation was racial peace—in other words, a withdrawal of the *negative* inducement to negotiate. Often one of the first conditions demanded by southern white leaders for the initiation of negotiations was a moratorium on demonstrations. There was no surer way for Negroes to lose their bargaining power than to accept this condition. Not only would the momentum of the demonstration be lost, but the leaders would find their positions compromised when they became members of any agency that was acceptable to the white community only if it promised to reduce tensions.

The types of protest that Wilson identified in his analysis were verbal, physical (sit-ins, picketing, and violence), economic (boy cotting), and political (voting reprisals). In most southern communities in 1960, the only form of protest that seemed sure of success was physical but nonviolent action. The successes that nonviolent direct action achieved stemmed chiefly from the tension and disorder that it created because of the propensity of segregationists to cooperate by responding with violent repression. So the tactic of nonviolent action became part of a strategy that invited conflict with local government.

· Coercive Public Protest

The most descriptive term that has been applied to the type of strategy that was emerging is "coercive public protest." This concept is used by a political scientist, David H. Bayley, in analyzing political protest in India.[13] Since Gandhi has been the model for civil rights strategists in the United States, it is not surprising that the analysis fits the Negro Revolution with little need for modification. According to Bayley, coercive public protest has three attributes: (1) it is aggregative; (2) it is public, as opposed to conspiratorial or clandestine; and (3) it imposes a constraint upon government by its presence and actions.[14] It may include legal forms (public meetings, boycotts, strikes, fasting) and illegal forms, both nonviolent (obstruction of thoroughfares and courting of arrest) and violent (rioting). The characteristic of coercive public protest that gives it a revolutionary potential, particularly in a democracy, is that "it represents a derogation from majority rule" and it is "a fundamental threat to the rule of law." [15] As Bayley says, coercive public protest is "a supplementary means for the suasion of government." [16] This means consists essentially of the negative inducement of which Wilson speaks—the creation of an emergency by the disruption of a social order. It is a means typically adopted by an aggrieved, powerless minority that feels that the legitimate channels of seeking redress are closed to it. Despite the promises of American democracy, Negro Americans had by 1960 come to the point of being such a minority, and this was the nature of the strategy they adopted.

· The Loss of Faith in White Government

The lack of faith in the willingness of the society to give Negroes relief from oppression through the ballot was voiced by James Farmer when he said, "I would not go so far as to say that the American white man is prepared not to survive in order to avoid giving Negroes equal rights, but I will say that I would not be prepared at the moment to put our cause to a general referendum in this country. I don't think we'd win it." [17]

The outburst of demonstrations in 1960, which Lomax labeled "The Negro Revolt," has been called a revolt against tokenism, against the legalism of the NAACP, and against the traditional Negro leadership class. While identifying all these targets, Lomax also pointed out the deeper significance of the shift to coercive public protest. He commented, "So far, the Deep South has thwarted our efforts toward school desegregation. But in the process they have done something even worse; they have destroyed the Negro's faith in the basic integrity of the white power structure." [18]

What he failed to add was that in losing faith in the integrity of the white power structure Negroes abandoned faith in government at the local and state levels, for this government was in the hands of that same white power structure.

Ostensibly the early demonstrations were directed not so much at government as at private businessmen who were engaged in discriminatory practices—restaurant owners, store managers, bus companies. But the real target was the power structure of the local community, including the city administration. Municipal officials repeatedly contributed to this definition of themselves as the resistance by intervening in behalf of beleaguered merchants; it was not just when demonstrations involved public facilities that they became involved. Demands by the leaders of demonstrations for the creation of *official* biracial committees also revealed that it was the political structure that was under attack. But by the same token mayors and city councilmen who would condone negotiations conducted by an *unofficial* committee would strongly resist demands for appointment of a biracial committee as part of the structure of city government.

This recalcitrance seems inconsistent with the fact that biracial committees rarely produced significant concessions for the militant Negro community. The inconsistency is resolved, however, when the biracial committee is seen as a symbol of Negro accession to a share of power in the local community, power that Negroes were unable to gain at the polls. For this same reason, few if any such committees, where they do exist, become anything more than advisory bodies. They are denied any real power by the elected officials who must create them.

Whether the official biracial committee became an issue or not, demonstrations were—and still are—aimed at the total white community, no matter what the nature of the specific targets. Desegregation, whether of one store or of the total community, was never really the issue; the issue was the distribution of power within the community. Negroes were attacking white supremacy all along the front.

· The Conflict Spreads North

While the eyes of the nation and often of the world were focused on the battle between Negro activists and southern white officials, the conflict was spreading outside the South. Along with the phrase "token integration," another new term was added to the vocabulary of the movement—"*de facto* segregation." Northern cities that had no segregation laws, that even prided themselves on their liberalism, were suddenly being compared to Alabama and Arkansas.

School boycotts protesting inferior conditions and *de facto* segregation were employed to force school boards into action. In New Rochelle, New York, such action was taken in the face of a referendum that had supported the school board by a margin of three to one.[19] The schools were not the only subject of Negro discontent. Philadelphia, later to be the scene of a bloodier battle, was in 1960 the locale of a series of boycotts that forced large corporations to change their hiring practices.

None of the problems of the Negro in the North—slum schools, unemployment, or residential segregation—were new, but there was an intensified awareness of them. Part of this new awareness reflected the economic cramp that developed during the latter part of the fifties, particularly in the burgeoning ghettoes of northern and western cities. Ideological cramp was being felt outside the South, too. The promise of a new equality for all Negroes, the struggle of southern Negroes to realize this promise, and the complacency of white America as the white South turned the new equality into token equality spread disillusionment into black neighborhoods all over the nation. Ironically, the plaintive and oft-repeated plea of white southerners that the problem of race relations was not just a southern problem, finally began to be heard —but only because it was now sounded by Negro voices.

In short order the biggest target of coercive public protest came to be the federal government itself. In the words of one observer, "throughout the cities of the South nonviolent demonstrations often seemed more precisely aimed at Pennsylvania Avenue and Capitol Hill than at the Albanys, Greenwoods or Shreveports where they were taking place. . . . By and large the approach seemed to be a short-circuited one that leaped quickly and brilliantly beyond the seemingly impenetrable conscience of a segregationist, fear-ridden populace to the power inherent in the national government." [20] This short-circuited approach reflected not only a lack of faith in the conscience of the populace, but also a loss of confidence in the sincerity of officials to whose election Negroes had contributed—including the President.

As has been observed earlier, the federal government was first perceived as an ally of the Negro protest movement. Had not the Supreme Court committed the power and dignity of the national government to the struggle for first-class citizenship? Had not President Eisenhower confirmed this commitment when he finally sent the troops to Little Rock? And had not John F. Kennedy given his blessing to the revolt in the provinces when he made his famous and perhaps fateful telephone call to the wife of Martin Luther King, Jr., while that leader was confined in a Georgia jail? There was at first good reason to believe that the federal government might indeed be the kind of ally that King says it should be when he asserts, "It is the obligation of government to move resolutely to the side of the freedom movement. There is a right and a wrong side in this conflict and the government does not belong in the middle." [21]

But this conception of the role of government vis-à-vis a militant and embattled social movement ignores the reality of how American government has operated—a reality summed up in the familiar adage, "Politics is the art of the possible." Not the reformer's dazzling vision of truth and right, but the cloudy compromise of diverse, sometimes contradictory, viewpoints determines where government will be. The sort of compromise that emerges reflects the relative power of the proponents of different viewpoints much more than it does the abstract merits of the conflicting arguments. Hence the position of government in America is usually near the middle. The gradualism and the compromises that result from the system of checks and balances may be mitigated when some crisis produces an emergency consensus. Or when a concentration of power neutralizes debate, extremism may characterize the position of American government. Such a concentration of power permitted radical white supremacy to characterize state and local government in the days of one party, lily-white politics. But neither in the South nor in the nation as a whole did the Negro protest movement have the political power to push government to the position of "extremism for love," which King, sounding like Barry Goldwater turned upside down, advocates as *"the* moral position." [22]

Not surprisingly the optimism engendered by the election of Kennedy in 1960 soon faded. In King's words:

> Then 1961 and 1962 arrived, with both parties marking time in the cause of justice. In the Congress, reactionary Republicans were still doing business with the Dixiecrats. And the feeling was growing among Negroes that the administration had oversimplified and underestimated the civil rights issue. President Kennedy, if not backing down, had backed away from the key pledge of his campaign—to wipe out housing discrimination immediately "with the stroke of a pen." [23]

Not only did the commitment of the federal government to the movement seem to be flagging, but King's own position as the top leader appeared insecure. His critics had been quick to call the stalemate that developed in Albany, Georgia, a defeat for him and for his Southern Christian Leadership Conference. By now, the cases of hundreds of demonstrators arrested on a variety of misdemeanor charges were dragging their way through the courts. Their heroic sacrifices had produced spotty and inconsistent results, all of which added up to more tokenism. New problems— Negro unemployment, expanding slums, school dropouts, increasing alienation—were being disclosed more rapidly than the old ones were progressing toward solution.

With the movement threatening to falter and lose its momentum, King resorted to the boldest use of the power of coercive public protest yet seen. Lerone Bennett, Jr.'s account of King's action at the beginning of 1963 reads, "As the Emancipation Proclamation Centennial drew near, King cast about for a Bastille, i.e., a key point that could yield more than a local or symbolic victory. With incredible boldness, he selected Birmingham which was widely regarded as an impregnable fortress of Jim Crow." [24]

Whether or not King envisioned the far-reaching effects of the confrontation at Birmingham, this is his own very accurate assessment of these effects, "The sound of the explosion in Birmingham reached all the way to Washington where the administration, which had firmly declared that civil rights legislation would have to be shelved for 1963, hastily reorganized its priorities and placed a strong civil rights bill at the top of the Congressional calendar." [25]

A sense of emergency, of national crisis, urgent enough to move even the legislative branch of the federal government to action had been created. The air of crisis continued for a year and a half, until the Civil Rights Act of 1964 was passed. It was sustained by hundreds of demonstrations, some involving clearly illegal obstruction, all over the nation; by the suicidal proclivity of the resistance to create martyrs and heroes for the movement; and by the assassination of President Kennedy. It was also sustained by the growing willingness of Negro leaders and intellectuals to hint darkly at the inevitability of a long hot summer or the fire next time if the demands of the movement were not met.

The Civil Rights Act of 1964, the most significant such law since Reconstruction days, was passed; but the air of crisis did not subside. Even as observers were expressing amazement at the extent of southern compliance with the public accommodations section, Negroes were rioting in the ghettoes of Philadelphia, Rochester, and New York. COFO (Council of Federated Organizations) workers in Mississippi were finding that in some counties attempting to

help Negroes to register as voters was considerably more dangerous than desegregating a lunch counter. While registrars proved as
ingenious as school board attorneys in circumventing the law.

There was a brief interlude of peace and optimism. In anticipa-
tion of the November presidential elections, Negro leaders called
for a temporary suspension of mass demonstrations and a "strategic turn toward political action." The Democratic landslide in
November was taken as "the expression of a majority liberal consensus." [26] Barry Goldwater, sitting in not-so-splendid isolation
with the electoral votes of only six states (five states of the Deep
South, and his home state of Arizona) seemed to symbolize the
defeat of white supremacy. In February, 1965, Bayard Rustin
wrote, "The decade spanned by the 1954 Supreme Court decision
on school desegregation and the Civil Rights Act of 1964 will undoubtedly be recorded as the period in which the legal foundati___s
of racism in America were destroyed." [27]

Yet less than two months later, and less than a year after President Johnson had signed the 1964 Act, the federal government was
faced with the necessity of intervening in another crisis in Alabama. This time the demonstrations dramatized the need for another civil rights law—a Voting Rights Act. Again, coercive public
protest produced change.

· The Illusion of Victory

On the night when the President of the United States said to a joint
session of the Congress and to the people of the nation, "And we
shall overcome," it would seem that the victory of the Negro Revolution was complete. The strategy of protest had proved successful.
Ten years earlier a President of the United States had refused to
express his agreement or disagreement with the desegregation rulings of the Supreme Court. Now another President used the rhetoric of the movement itself in demanding action from the legisla-

tive branch. When five months later, he signed the Voting Rights Bill into law, he proclaimed that it represented a victory for Negro leadership.

What made this victory even more remarkable was that this President was a southern white Democrat who had stood loyally with the congressional bloc for years. But in August, 1965, Louis Lomax said of this same man, "Let the truth be told: Lyndon Baines Johnson is now the number one 'Negro' leader!" [28]

Lomax said this cynically and somewhat sadly because he recognized that the Johnson administration and its program symbolized both a victory and a dilemma for the Negro Revolution. The victory that the revolution had achieved consisted of securing a white liberal government. In Crane Brinton's terms, "the rule of the moderates" had begun.[29] As Rustin had already observed, the 1964 law seemed to have destroyed the legal foundations of racism. The Economic Opportunity Act and the War on Poverty, furnished the tools for attacking the cumulative effects of racism. The Voting Rights Act seemed to provide the basis for even more effective Negro participation in what Rustin described as "a coalition of progressive forces which becomes the *effective* political majority in the United States . . . Negroes, trade unionists, liberals, and religious groups." [30]

As Brinton observes, there is, however, "an almost organic weakness in the position of the moderates" when they come to power in the early stages of a revolution. "They are placed between two groups, the disgruntled but not yet silenced conservatives and the confident, aggressive extremists." As a result, the rule of the moderates constitutes, he suggests, a relatively brief honeymoon, which loses its charm as "the moderates find themselves losing the credit they had gained as opponents of the Old Regime, and taking on more and more of the discredit innocently associated by the hopeful many with the status of heir to the Old Regime." [31]

How soon the bright promise of the white liberal government of

Lyndon B. Johnson began to pale is suggested by the bitter remarks of a Negro writer, Simeon Booker, in August 1965, less than a year after the Great Society had been proclaimed as the new American dream. "Everywhere," he wrote, "white opposition has braked the desegregation speed of the Great Society program and controlled its impact. . . . Comprising a huge civil rights network with emphasis on percentages, gobbledegook and vast amounts of paper work, the race relations program is geared for the majority white with a message of love and tolerance and for the Negro to qualify for openings." [32]

This was a harbinger of a theme that would grow stronger in the following year. This is the thesis that the enemy of the Negro protest movement is not primarily the die-hard conservatives of the southern resistance, but the liberal Establishment, including the federal government itself. It was a thesis against which Rustin had warned when he wrote:

> It has become fashionable in some no-win Negro circles to decry the white liberal as the main enemy (his hypocrisy is what sustains racism) ; by virtue of this reverse recitation of the reactionary's litany (liberalism leads to socialism, which leads to communism) the Negro is left in majestic isolation, except for a tiny band of fervent white initiates. [33]

• The Growth of a Revolutionary Definition

Some social movements are popularly defined as dangerous and revolutionary from their inception because of the values they espouse and their open quest for power. This happens when the early leaders of the movement through an excess either of idealism or optimism state their objectives too bluntly and too soon. Thus the Nazi movement almost died aborning when Hitler attempted the Beer Hall Putsch before he had built a broad base of support, particularly in the army and in the business world. During the years after his imprisonment the future dictator changed his strategy to a careful wooing and deception of militarists and financiers who had earlier regarded his program as a threat to their own interests. He abandoned all thoughts of a coup d'état and determined "to make his revolution after achieving political power." [34]

In the United States, socialist movements have encountered persistent, crippling opposition because the very term "socialist" evokes for many Americans images of violent revolution, confiscation of private property, and political dictatorship. The fact that the Socialist party has always advocated reform by constitutional means has not removed the aura of danger that surrounds it. But many of the same reforms it has proposed have been accepted as respectable and nonrevolutionary when advocated by the major political parties.

Except in the South, the Negro protest movement was not initially defined as revolutionary by the white public. Focusing its attack on the openly discriminatory segregation laws of the South, attacking these laws through the courts, it fit the pattern of many successful reform movements. Like other movements that have become revolutions, it appealed to the traditional values of equality, freedom, and respect for law. It cast the southern white resistance in the role of the revolutionaries. The surveys conducted by Louis Harris have shown that there is majority white support, at least on a verbal level, for such Negro goals as the right to vote, decent housing, and equality in employment.[35] In 1963, he found that even in the South a large majority of whites felt that Negroes should be guaranteed these rights. How, then, might the movement come to be defined as revolutionary by the white public?

While Harris continued to find majority white support for Negro goals, he found widespread opposition to the methods being used by Negroes to advance their cause. As has been pointed out before, in 1963 he found two-to-one opposition to lunch counter sit-ins, five-to-three against picketing of stores, and over ten-to-one opposition to lie-downs in front of trucks at construction sites.[36] He observed, "These very demonstrations appear to have driven home the whole point of the Negro protest. But the majority view of the whites was clearly that the Negroes were pressing too hard, asking for too much." [37]

Two years later, Harris found even stronger condemnation of demonstrations. He found that nationwide 62 percent of whites felt that demonstrations had hurt the cause of Negro rights more than they had helped.[38] In another survey conducted a few months later he found the alleged fact that "Negroes are pushing ahead too fast" ranked third among things that whites would like to see corrected in the United States.[39]

Here is revealed one of the major dilemmas of the Negro protest movement. As one of Harris' subjects said, "The whites would forget us quick if we didn't keep bringing our situation to their attention." [40] Much of white support for Negro rights appears to be lip service, an approval of rights without a corresponding commitment to do anything to grant them. But the strategy that Negroes have found to be effective in moving the society to effective action also threatens the secure, orderly world of white America. As white people feel threatened, pushed, and even overpowered by demands for rapid change, they come closer to defining the movement, whatever its goals may be, as dangerous and truly revolutionary. In turn, their preference for moderation and gradualism convinces Negroes that a lessening of protest would mean the end of progress. Thus the cycle that leads a social movement into increasing reliance upon aggressive displays of power is set in motion.

There may be a number of explanations for white disapproval of the strategy of protest. A very simple one would be the strength of the conviction that in a democracy change should be brought through public debate and legislative deliberation, not through direct action and emergency legislation. While Negroes are not the only group who have engaged in coercive public protest in order to hasten social change, there is always a suggestion of danger to the whole democratic process when this strategy is used. It is an emergency measure, to be employed when the will of the majority is too slow to respond to the critical needs of a minority. But the success of such emergency tactics poses a threat to the normal processes of majority rule. As Bayley observes, "Coercive public protest, if allowed to go unrestrained, will be more widely imitated and become an even greater rival to the processes of peaceful change through democratic government." [41] Perhaps many white Americans who do not feel the desperation of the demonstrators even though they approve in theory of their cause experience an intuitive fear that what Bayley describes might happen. The recent adoption of the tactics of the civil rights movement by the student movement and the peace movement is likely to heighten this fear.

A strategy of power and protest also places another demand on the white person that may be threatening to him. When Negroes confront segregated institutions with their bodies, a commitment to people, not just to theories, is demanded even of bystanders. Despite the presence of white supporters in demonstrations, the confrontation is fundamentally between Negroes and whites. To align himself psychologically with Negroes picketing a white store, or marching on a white courthouse, or parading in a white neighborhood may be very difficult for a white person who cannot imagine himself engaging in such conduct and who feels that the white storeowner, government official, or homeowner is more nearly his kind than are the demonstrators. As demonstrations spread from the South to other regions, this type of alignment on a racial rather than an ideological basis is likely to increase. As Oscar Handlin suggests, "Toward the Negroes, the suburbanites exhibit goodwill conditioned by distance." [42] Since 1963, the sense of distance has been rapidly decreasing as open housing has become a prime issue. Charles Silberman declared in 1964:

> And so the North is finally beginning to face the reality of race. In the process, it is discovering animosities and prejudices that had been hidden in the recesses of the soul. For a brief period following the demonstrations in Birmingham in the spring of 1963—a very brief period—it appeared that the American conscience had been touched; a wave of sympathy for the Negro and of revulsion over white brutality seemed to course through the nation. But then the counteraction set in, revealing a degree of anti-Negro prejudice and hatred that surprised even the most sophisticated observers. [43]

Hence we should not overlook the possibility that disapproval of the tactics of the Negro Revolution is, even outside the South, merely a rationalization that masks underlying disapproval of the goals of the movement. The evidence of history bears out the validity of Douglass' conviction that Negro rights could never be secure so long as they depended on the benevolence of white men. Myrdal observed the ambivalence of which white Americans are capable as they approve the abstract values of the American creed yet justify the differential treatment of Negroes. The strategy of the Negro Revolution, more than anything else in American history, has demanded that this ambivalence be resolved so that all men does include Negro Americans. Disapproval of this strategy may be merely the latest way of affirming the unspoken conviction that America was meant to be a white man's country.

Whatever the reason, white Americans seem to give lip service to the values of the Negro movement while condemning the strategy that has proved effective in promoting these values. At the same time they have shown little initiative in promoting these values by other means, thereby making the strategy of protest necessary. Not by their words but by their lack of action, they have defined the demands of the Negro protest as unworthy of serious consideration. They have forced the movement into reliance on a strategy of power that has been condemned. This implicit definition of the movement as dangerous has made it revolutionary and has given the advantage to those leaders who argue that only protest will produce change.

V

The Federal Government:
The New Enemy

By the summer of 1965, the strategy of protest had become clearly dominant in the civil rights movement. Prominent Negro leaders flying to Alabama to march for a few of the fifty miles from Selma to Montgomery symbolized the importance of participation in coercive public protest as an essential credential for leadership. Although there was optimism that new federal laws and the voter registration drives would make possible the shift from protest to politics, this was only a dream, not a reality. The moratorium on demonstrations requested in 1964 by Dr. King and Roy Wilkins, but not by James Farmer of CORE and John Lewis of SNCC, could be regarded as no more than an unstable truce; the white liberal government of Lyndon B. Johnson was still on trial with Negroes.

In 1963 Bayard Rustin had aptly characterized the strategy of the revolution when he wrote, "The use of the 'black body' against injustice is necessary as a means of creating social disruption and dislocation precisely because the accepted democratic channels have been denied the Negro." [1]

While Rustin had been writing about demonstrations in the South, it has been seen that the federal government had also become a target of the strategy of power. Indeed, the more the federal government, through civil rights laws and executive pronouncements, committed itself to a policy of intervention in local power struggles, the more it made itself a target. In April, 1966, Negro farm laborers from Mississippi camped in Lafayette Square symbolizing how clearly the White House had become a target of protest.

While the theme of protest remained dominant, so also did the theme of nonviolence. Martin Luther King, Jr., was still the symbol of militant Negro leadership. But the scale of militancy had shifted, and King now appeared to be near the center on that scale. The NAACP found itself being described as respectable, even conservative, and being bracketed with the National Urban League. Since the freedom rides of 1960, CORE had regained some of its luster as a symbol of nonviolent resistance to discrimination. Indeed, in November, 1964, Martin Mayer of the *Saturday Evening Post* had labeled CORE "The Shocktroops of the Negro Revolt." [2] But the Student Non-Violent Coordinating Committee, the newest of the protest organizations, had gained the reputation of being the most aggressive. While both of these organizations still espoused nonviolence, their allegiance to it was now clearly based on its tactical value, not its moral superiority. Mayer said of the tactics of CORE:

> CORE's "nonviolence" has sometimes taken on a character which Gandhi might have had trouble recognizing. In San Francisco, a CORE group has attacked a chain of supermarkets by loading shopping carts with groceries, then dumping them on the floor around the cashiers' tables. In St. Louis, pickets have blocked access to a bank that had refused to hire Negroes. In Cleveland, CORE members have thrown themselves in front of a bulldozer working on the site of what would be a segregated school; one of them, a young white clergyman, was killed when the driver backed the bulldozer away, not knowing someone was behind him. In New York, CORE members have dumped garbage in the roadway to block a major bridge at rush hour, chained themselves to

construction cranes, and jammed the stairs to a union office to keep the officers from going in or out. It was Brooklyn CORE that tried unsuccessfully to tie up traffic on the roads leading to the World's Fair; and it was a congeries of CORE chapters that briefly barricaded the doors to both national political conventions.[3]

· The Theme of Power

Distrust of whites and displacement of white co-workers from positions of leadership was progressing in these organizations, and the theme of power was being enunciated more clearly. In his annual report to the CORE national convention in July, 1965, James Farmer declared:

> The major war now confronting us is aimed at harnessing the awesome political potential of the black community in order to effect basic social and economic changes for all Americans, to alter meaningfully the lives of the Black Americans, and to bring about a real equality of free men. . . .
> This job cannot be done for us by the government. In the first place, the establishments—Federal, State and Local—have too much built-in resistance to fundamental change. Any establishment by definition seeks its own perpetuation and rejects that which threatens it.[4]

Still, open rejection of the American social system as a white man's society and the justification of violence, at least in self-defense, remained the property of groups that appeared to be so "far out" as to be beyond the fringes of the movement. The Black Muslims and the defectors who had followed Malcolm X out of the sect were the best known proponents of black nationalism and retaliatory violence. Robert F. Williams, expelled from the NAACP in 1959 for declaring that Negroes should meet violence with violence and now a fugitive from both state and federal warrants, was broadcasting appeals for revolution from Cuba. His remoteness from the North American continent and from the attention of the American public, white and Negro, seemed to suggest that the Negro Revolution included no place for revolutionaries of his ilk. While Williams seemed to have no significant and certainly no visible following in the United States, the black ghettoes of the major American cities contained numerous splinter groups that were as blatantly anti-white-American and just as prone to violence as this expatriate might have asked. Even in the Deep South, the Deacons for Defense and Justice had adopted vigilant tactics to defend Negroes when the law did not do so. The Deacons had no ideology except the right of self-defense, but they had clearly rejected King's philosophy of nonviolence. Furthermore, they had received the endorsement of one of the major leadership groups, CORE.

· A "Cool Summer"?

All of the above seemed to represent eddies thrown off from the mainstream of the protest movement, not portents of significant future developments. The quiet of the spring and early summer of 1965 seemed to give the lie to prophets of intensified conflict. The riots of the notorious long hot summer of 1964 had not been repeated and as August came it appeared that this might indeed prove to be a "cool summer." Not that protests had stopped; SNCC, CORE, and SCLC workers and their local allies were again confronting southern resistance in the deep southern states. Bogalusa, Louisiana, remained a battleground between nonviolent civil rights workers on one side, and the Ku Klux Klan and local government on the other. Outside the South, civil rights demonstrators were also in sporadic conflict with government during the spring and summer of 1964. In Chicago, the police were providing protection for peaceful marchers, but were arresting demonstrators who carried the tactic of social disruption to the point of lying down on downtown streets during the rush hour. School Superintendent Benjamin C. Willis and Mayor Richard Daley were the targets; school integration was the immediate issue. In Milwaukee, demonstrators blocked school buses, and in Springfield, Massachusetts, CORE members staged a sit-in in the office of the school superintendent. In Brooklyn, there was a demonstration in a courtroom when supporters of the Reverend Milton A. Galamison objected to his conviction on charges growing out of a February school boycott. In New York City, intensification of demands for a civilian police review board underlined the growing distrust of the police by Negroes in that city as in the rest of the nation. Nor did the federal government itself go unscathed. In June, twelve Mississippi Negroes participating in a SNCC demonstration against the Mississippi delegation in the House of Representatives were arrested for refusing to leave the office of the House clerk.

Yet there were positive signs for optimism in addition to the mere absence of Negro rioting. Early in June, President Johnson in his address at Howard University had promised to carry the struggle for equality beyond the level of equality of opportunity to the goal of equality as a fact. He announced that he would call a White House conference in the fall, the theme of which would be "to fulfill these rights." In July, an administration report on the effect of the first year of the 1964 Civil Rights Act claimed the act was well on its way to the accomplishment of its principal aim, an end of divisions in American society. The attack on job discrimination began when the Equal Employment Opportunities Commission began accepting complaints under Title VII. The War on Poverty had been launched. Early in August, the Voting Rights Bill of 1965 was signed into law, and federal voting registrars immediately went into action in nine southern counties. The Leadership Conference on Civil Rights had acclaimed the Bill as "altogether a superior piece of legislation." Even the House Un-American Activities Committee, whatever its motives, was preparing to open the investigation of the Ku Klux Klan as it had promised following the slaying of Mrs. Viola Liuzzo near Selma, Alabama.

· The Los Angeles Riots

Then in mid-August, the riots in South Los Angeles ripped aside this thin facade of peace and progress. Although this massive eruption of Negro violence is a part of very recent history, its significance as a turning point in the Negro Revolution is already established. This significance arises not so much from the nature of the riots as from what they revealed about the movement and from the reactions to them.

Although these riots dwarfed previous outbursts in the extent of their destructiveness, they were not without precedent. The riots of Harlem, Rochester, and Philadelphia during the summer of 1964 were of essentially the same quality, involving Negro attacks on property and on the police. They had made it clear that in spite of the urgings of Martin Luther King, Jr., Negro protests were not synonymous with nonviolent demonstrations. The same type of outbursts had occurred in Jacksonville, Florida, in 1960. The capacity of the inhabitants of the black ghettoes to resort to violent conflict had been demonstrated even earlier in the long-forgotten Harlem riot of 1943. There is a striking similarity in that Harlem riot and the Watts riot. Both were triggered by conflicts between a white policeman and Negroes, including women, charged with disorderly conduct. Lee and Humphrey, writing about the Negroes in the Harlem riots, might have been writing about the Negroes of Los Angeles when they said, "They looted, destroyed property, and badgered police out of sheer desperation and 'cussedness' for being outcast members of a degraded caste in the only country they know and love, a country in which they have lived for a greater average period of time than their white neighbors." [5]

There had been warnings, too, that such explosions might replace the violence of whites in the South as the major threat to racial peace in the country. James B. Conant had warned of "dynamite in the cities." [6] Killian and Grigg had written in 1964:

> But the lower-class Negro community, becoming more homogeneously lower class as the Negro middle class is able to escape from it, may prove to be more than simply a refuge where the disadvantaged may nurse their broken dreams. . . . With disappointment and despair come bitterness, hostility, and reckless aggression. The Negro community is also a reservoir of followers awaiting to be mobilized by the new Negro men of power . . . "conflict leaders" who find their strength not in the ideals or the guilt of white Americans caught in the American Dilemma, not in the approval and the concessions they are able to gain from paternalistic white leaders, but in the frustration, hostility, and need for identity of millions of Negroes.[7]

Shortly before his death, and immediately after the long hot summer of 1964, Malcolm X had predicted, "More and worse riots will erupt. The black man has seen the white man's underbelly of guilty fear." [8]

While the leaders of the major protest organizations did not talk in terms of more riots as did this defiant revolutionary, they did not soften the vehemence of the slogan "Freedom Now." The sociological generalization that a revolution does not decelerate but accelerates as gains are made had been translated into a warning to the white power structure to expect more, not less, trouble. In 1963 Kenneth Clark in an interview for the conservative *U. S. News and World Report* had spoken directly to this power structure in the following exchange:

QUESTION: Many people express puzzlement over this: They say Negroes at this time are making progress in many ways, and they wonder why, as Negroes make more progress, they become more militant.

ANSWER: One of the reasons people don't understand this is that they don't understand history. No totally oppressed people ever revolt or rebel. Now I use your word "revolt" in this sense: The Negroes' revolution comes as a consequence of what white liberals call progress. The closer a human being gets to a goal, obviously the more restive he gets in wanting that goal.[9]

The sociologist Robin M. Williams, Jr., a long-time and perceptive observer of race relations, had diagnosed the difficulties of keeping Negro protest nonviolent in a paper delivered less than a year before the Los Angeles riots. Against the background of the riots of 1964, he said:

. . . the growth of deep despair and alienation among the low-income, low-education strata of the urban Negro ghettoes has been the prelude to the predictable outbreak of more and more "expressive violence." Unlike the well-disciplined, highly purposive and remarkably patient behavior of earlier organized protests, the emergence of diffuse terrorism and rioting is non-instrumental and chaotic.[10]

Almost prophetically he went on to say:

It is difficult to sustain the nonviolent character of nonviolent social movements intended to substantially change the existing subordination and segregation of a minority group, especially if the movement is successful in initial attacks on limited objectives, and then confronts hardening resistance to broader and more crucial aims. When objectives are limited, the tactics can be such as to clearly show a direct connection between means and ends, e.g., the sit-ins to desegregate lunch counters. Selective pressure on the sensitive "pocketbook nerve" of business enterprises by a highly selected and well-disciplined organization often has brought specific, restricted gains. But as hopes rise, such gains may be seen as illusory by those who fail to benefit and whose problems of employment and status worsen rather than lessen. Cynical alienation gains increased frustration. Hostility is more freely expressed, and the likelihood grows of *expressive* aggression. Actual outbreaks assume a run-away character and release a great variety of hostile and opportunistically predatory forces.[11]

The Los Angeles riots, and smaller outbursts in Chicago, Springfield, Massachusetts, and Philadelphia later the same week, constituted such expressive aggression. It is not necessary, however, to view these riots as deliberately planned protests to define them as part of the movement. While the rioters could not individually give a coherent explanation of why they were rioting—they were acting, not philosophizing—the context in which the riots occurred suggests an explanation on the sociological level.

· The Background for Watts

There were the conditions of deprivation in the ghetto that since the riots have come to be widely recognized as very real grievances of the people. Frustration, alienation, and lack of identity, all accentuated by feelings of relative deprivation, must be regarded as psychological factors that created a readiness for individuals to give vent to what Williams called "expressive hostility." Such expressive hostility has burst out in Watts and other Negro slums daily in the form of small acts of aggression against representatives of the dominant group or against other minority group members. But it was the collective support given this expressive hostility, permitting the spread and intensification of it in reckless defiance of police power, that made the outbursts an instance of collective behavior that was more than just another race riot. Directed against the power of America's second largest city and, in the end, against the military forces of the state, the riot took on the character of an insurrection.

In sociological language Robert Blauner described this insurrection as "the crystalization of community identity through a nationalistic outburst against the society felt as dominating and oppressive. The spirit of the Watts rioters appears similar to that of anticolonial crowds demonstrating against foreign masters. . . ." [12] Blauner also argues that the riots must not be viewed as "a Los Angeles version of a mass civil rights protest," on the grounds that the organization was too loose. [13]

· The Crowd and Negro Leaders

It is quite clear that this and similar collective outbursts are not part of the civil rights movement, but Watts made it inescapably clear that they were part of the Negro Revolution. The civil rights movement as King, Wilkins, and the other established leaders would have it would stop short of coercive public protest that is violent. They did not want the Negro masses to burn Watts any more than the bourgeoisie of the early days of the French Revolution intended that the Paris mobs destroy the Bastille or storm the Palace of Versailles. But the rioters of August, 1965, were demonstrating that they, too, were part of the revolution, and on their own terms. They were a crowd, not an organized, disciplined group of demonstrators. Watts marked the point at which the violent Negro crowd entered the Negro Revolution. The rioters did not create the revolution; they declared themselves "in" a revolutionary movement that was already going on. The negative, almost aimless behavior of the crowd, and the substitution of "Burn, Baby, Burn" for the specific, negotiable demands with which the civil rights organizations justify their demonstrations, both signify that the riots marked a turning point in the revolution. The masses had joined the revolution in the way that Trotsky had described when he wrote, "The masses go into a revolution not with a prepared plan of social reconstruction, but with a sharp feeling that they cannot endure the old regime. Only the guiding layers of a class have a political program, and even this still requires the test of events, and the approval of the masses." [14]

The revolution itself was part of the situation that led to the addition of rioting to the tactics of protest. Thomas Pettigrew has summed up the impact of the earlier stages of the revolution in creating relative deprivation among such peoples whom he calls "the other Negro America."

> Now constituting perhaps two-thirds of all Negroes this other Negro America has not as yet been significantly touched by present racial adjustments. Nor has it had any increased contact with white Americans in recent years; rather, it slips further and further into the depths of "the dark ghetto" and its own desperate despair. Its hopes were raised in the 1950s; but now it cannot even rationalize personal failure entirely in racial terms, for *Ebony* bulges each month with evidence that "the affluent Negro America" is making rapid strides.[15]

After the 1964 disorders, the leaders of the civil rights movement had recognized their neglect of this other Negro America. They had not been able to move fast enough, however, to improve their plight nor to bring them into the movement. Martin Luther King realized fully how much he and others had failed when Negroes in Watts jeered him and told him to go back to the other side of town.

· The Issue of Law

But the relationship of the earlier phases of the revolution to this new development involves even more than the raising and dashing of hopes. Two other factors were involved. One was the relationship of law to change in racial patterns. The other was the power of Negroes vis-à-vis whites in American society.

The elite vanguard of the Negro Revolution, the NAACP, had set the stage for a legal conflict when it won the school case and subsequent cases involving other tax-supported facilities. Armed now with the law of the land, this organization sought to keep the conflict within the legal arena. One of the first indications that its efforts would be doomed was the formation of the short-lived National Association for the Advancement of White People, which rallied mobs of defiant white people to oppose legally imposed desegregation in Washington, Baltimore, and Delaware in the fall of 1954. The bombing of the high school in Clinton, Tennessee, and the attacks on the Little Rock pioneers soon validated this grim impression. Southern white politicians, reviving the doctrine of interposition and denouncing the Supreme Court as communistic, gave an implicit blessing to the extralegal tactics.

The Montgomery bus boycott and the sit-ins revealed that Negroes as well as whites were prepared to utilize forms of power other than legal compulsion. While King and CORE advocated nonviolence, they still took the conflict to the streets. More important, the new emphasis on civil disobedience instead of mere test cases fostered a growing disrespect for legal processes. It should be noted that both the movement and the resistance remained ready to acclaim and utilize the law when court rulings at any echelon favored their respective cause. Yet both were ready to appeal to the higher law, defying even the federal establishment, if the tide turned against them.

And from 1954, there was deliberate defiance of law at all levels. Negroes and their white allies violated local and state laws, particularly those alleged to protect private property, hoping that they would be declared unconstitutional. White segregationists took the lead in refusing to abide by federal laws. For ten years before

Watts, newspapers and television presented to the public a live story that often resembled a gargantuan T.V. western. Heroes and villains, good guys and bad guys, decided for themselves which laws were just. Local and state law officers often improvised the law south of Washington like frontier marshals. To white segregationists, these modern Wyatt Earps and their vigilante allies were the heroes. But to millions of Negroes the villains of the daily newscasts were the law as represented by Governor Ross Barnett, Alabama Patrol Chief Al Lingo, or Sheriff Jim Clark.

It was easy for Negroes in the ghettoes outside the South to find confirmation of the belief that the police represented the enemy. Real and alleged police brutality, ranging from unwarranted violence to unwitting use of the language of prejudice, became an issue that overrode concern for law and order. The tragic fact was that law and justice came to be opposites, not synonyms, for millions of Negroes, particularly the poorer ones. Conservative white Americans began to display a surprising and belated concern for law and order. The attempt was made to introduce the theme of "violence in the streets" into the 1964 presidential race. With each outbreak of Negro violence, no matter how remote its relation to the protest movement, ominous warnings were sounded about the disrespect for law engendered by civil rights leaders.

Though civil rights leaders may have accentuated a mood of disrespect for law among Negroes, they had not created it. In speaking of the duty to disobey unjust laws, King and others had only elevated to a higher plane something that already existed on the level of cynicism. Twenty years before Myrdal had observed of Negroes in the South:

> They will not feel confidence in, and loyalty toward, a legal order which is entirely out of their control and which they sense to be inequitable and merely part of the system of caste suppression. Solidarity then develops easily in the Negro

group, a solidarity against the law and the police. The arrested Negro often acquires the prestige of a victim, a martyr, or a hero, even when he is simply a criminal.[16]

In *An American Dilemma*, Myrdal concluded that "there is in the North no special problem of getting justice for Negroes, outside the general one of improving the working of the machinery of the law for the equal protection of the rights of poor and uneducated people." [17] By the sixties, however, thousands of southern Negroes had crowded into urban ghettoes in every region. The improvement of the working of the machinery of the law had not kept pace with the pressures of population density, inferior education, and underemployment. The drastic upgrading of the police in terms of education, salary, and prestige, which Myrdal had identified as a crucial factor in reducing racial tensions, had not been achieved in time to prevent the police from becoming one of the primary targets of the Negro Revolution. During the summers of 1964 through 1967, rioting broke out in cities of the North and West as well as of the South, as Negroes defined members of their race as victims, martyrs, or heroes when they were arrested, just as Myrdal had described.

So disrespect for law, which seemed to be for the white man and against the Negro, was not new. What was new was the *sense of power* that the early successes of the revolution had created. The nonviolent demonstrations of SCLC, CORE, and SNCC and the threats of the Black Muslims had not solved the bitter problems of the Negro masses, but they had shown that the Negro minority could strike terror into the hearts of the white majority. They had produced concessions from white people, even though the triumph of winning these concessions had soon turned to despair because they were never enough. Watts and the other riots reflected no clearly formulated demand for new concessions. They did reflect the basic truth that Negroes, mobilized in ghettoes to an extent never before experienced and made confident by earlier victories, were no longer afraid of white power. Within a few months after Watts, they would begin to proclaim their faith in Black Power.

Yet it must be emphasized that the riots were all spontaneous. In spite of assiduous searches, no evidence has been produced that any Negro leaders have deliberately set off riots as part of the strategy of coercive public protest. In Watts, Martin Luther King and Dick Gregory were reviled by the crowd and told to go back to the other side of town; in the confusion Gregory was hit by a bullet. How, then, can it be said that rioting became part of the strategy of the Negro Revolution?

· The Reaction of Negro Leaders

The established Negro leaders, whether of the old elite or of the newest, most militant generation, had to react to the riots even though they did not desire them. It was their response to the violence of the crowd that brought illegal rioting into the mainstream of the revolution and made it part of the strategy of protest. This response was essentially one of using the riots as a weapon of protest even while deploring them. There was little else that the leaders could do if they were to preserve even a semblance of leadership.

With relationship to the people who composed the crowds, these spokesmen for the Negro's cause were what George Rudé has called "outside leaders." [18] Deriving his propositions from the relationship of the *sans culottes* to the Jacobin leaders in the French Revolution, he points out that men who provide the ideological background for the activities of the crowd are seldom drawn from the same social class as their followers. The deliberate and rather self-conscious adoption of overalls as the "uniform" of SNCC reflects the fact that even these militant protest organizations have a class barrier to overcome in order to reach the Negro people. According to Rudé's analysis, the consequence of this sort of separation in the French Revolution was:

> By his position "outside the crowd," the leader was always in danger of losing his control over a protracted period, or of seeing his ideas adapted to purposes other than those he had intended. . . .
>
> The leaders (and this was particularly the case in a protracted movement like the French Revolution) were at times compelled, in order to maintain their authority, to trim or adapt their policies to meet the wishes of the crowd.[19]

Confronted with the riots of 1964 and 1965, the outside leaders of the Negro Revolution theoretically had two choices. One was to condemn the riots and the rioters in unequivocal terms as being without legal or moral justification. Yet this was no choice at all. While a Negro leader might afford to deplore lawbreaking, he could not with impunity or honesty deny the grievances of the rioters. To do so would be to reject the inhabitants of the ghettoes and to align himself with the white resistance. He would be in a position of accepting their definition of the crucial issue as law and order, not justice and equality.

The live option was to interpret the riots in terms of what were perceived as the underlying causes. But faults that could be ascribed to irresponsibility on the part of the rioters themselves were inadmissible as causes. Already the major civil rights organizations were distressed by the implications of the riots for their own position. After Watts, James Farmer commented, "Civil rights organizations have failed. No one had any roots in the ghetto." [20] The ultimate causes had to be sought outside the ghetto—in American society itself. Thus the riots were interpreted as symptoms of brutality, segregated housing, segregated schools, economic exploitation of ghetto residents, tokenism in employment practices, the indifference of white politicians, and the inadequacy of the federal antipoverty program. The line between explanation and justification was a thin one. As Rudé has suggested, ". . . leaders, far from exercising undisputed control over their followers, might be overruled by them, and, in a sense, the role of leader and follower would be reversed!"[21] Martin Luther King denounced vigorously the mood reflected by "Burn, Baby, Burn," but he embraced the issues that the physical attack on the ghetto symbolized. He moved his base of operations to the city of Chicago, and he announced that his next goal was to "end the slums."

To explain the riots in terms that condemned not the rioters but the society that had created their grievances carried another implication that brought the riots even more definitely within the strategy of the revolution. The implication was that if these grievances were not corrected, and soon, there would be more riots. It is at this point that the magnitude of the Watts riot becomes significant. The amount of destruction that actually occurred and the size of the forces required to end the carnage generated a nightmare in which an entire American city would be destroyed because the fires could not be checked. Once this terrifying specter was glimpsed it could not be forgotten. Massive, violent racial conflict was no longer just a theoretical possibility among the speculations of sociologists. Part of the terror had been a reality. No longer could the urgency of the Negro's demands be discussed without conjuring up the image of another Watts. Within a few days after the rioting in Los Angeles, Charles Evers, the top NAACP leader in Mississippi, warned the citizens of Natchez that if the demonstrations he was leading did not produce results the kind of thing that had happened in Watts might occur in their city.[22] He made it clear that he did not advocate such a tactic, but he predicted that frustrated, angry Negroes might use it. A year later Francisco Rodriguez, an NAACP lawyer and one of the forgotten heroes of the early legal battles, warned the citizens of Tampa, Florida, "We stand on the threshold of the same riots that took place in Cleveland, Atlanta and other cities." [23] His prophesy was tragically realized when Tampa erupted in violence in the late spring of 1967.

Neither the actuality of Watts nor the dire prophecies of more riots to come were sufficient to forestall the spread of ghetto violence. In the summer of 1966, there were riots in eighteen areas. By mid-August of 1967, there had been riots in thirty-one cities. The deaths, injuries, and property damage in Newark almost equalled the record of Los Angeles. Later in July, Detroit became the new symbol of the nightmare of the cities. The forty-two deaths in that city exceeded the toll in Los Angeles. As in Watts, most of the victims—all but eight—were Negroes. Detroit achieved another distinction: not only the National Guard but also regulars from the army's strategic reserve were called in to restore order.

The position of responsible Negro leaders in the mid-sixties came to have a striking resemblance to that of moderate white southerners during the previous decade. Neither advocated extralegal violence; both found themselves using the possibility of its occurrence as part of their strategic appeal to the opposition and to the uncommitted public. King reflected the dilemma of these leaders in statements made before a national television audience in September, 1966. [24] First, there was his own rejection of the tactics of violence: "For the Negro to turn from nonviolence would be both impractical and immoral." But then came the note of sympathy and understanding for those who in desperation turn to violence: "A riot is the language of the unheard. . . ." Next came the warning: "We don't have long. The mood of the Negro community is one of urgency. . . ." And, finally, in response to the question, "How long must we expect such outbursts to go on?," the placing of the blame: "White America will determine how long it will be!"

A dozen years before, white attorneys and journalists had pleaded with the NAACP and the United States Supreme Court to relent in their demands for immediacy so as to save the South from a race war. Now Negro leaders were pleading with white America to abandon its posture of gradualism and tokenism in order to save the nation from a race war. Both attested to their condemnation of open, violent conflict, but both disclaimed their power to prevent it. To both, the only answer in this conflict situation was for the other side to surrender.

· The Gain for the Radicals

In both cases, the unanticipated and undesired consequences were to allow the radical leaders to upstage the moderate leaders. This is partly a function of the selective attention of the commercial press, which finds more news value in wars and rumors of war than in long-range proposals for social reform. It is also partly a function of the fears and the need for justification of the opposition. The already existing ambivalence of many white Americans who would agree that Negroes had legitimate grievances but would argue that they were going too fast and using the wrong methods could be resolved. Every outburst of ghetto violence could be seized on as evidence that the civil rights movement had stirred up unreasonable aspirations and violent passions in a people who were "not ready" for full participation in a society based on respect for law and order! So Stokely Carmichael came to have a far greater fascination for white Americans than did King, or Wilkins, or Young. He confirmed their fears and justified their righteous indignation.

The nature of the conflict situation also gave an advantage to the newest radicals, the leaders who did not shrink from the prospect of violence. These were the Negro spokesmen, Carmichael and H. Rap Brown on the national level, others known only within their local ghettoes, who did not dilute their expressions of sympathy for the rioters with affirmation of the virtues of nonviolence and respect for law. They justified violence itself, with the proviso only that it should be retaliatory. Carmichael urged his audiences, "If a white man puts his hand on you, break his arm!" And Brown, in the days immediately following the riots in Detroit, was to cry repeatedly for revenge against the "honkies." The advantage lay with leaders of this type because they approved a new tactic in a protracted conflict, a revolution that had not been decisively crushed but had not achieved its crucial goals.

· The New Cutting Edge

The old tactics of legalism and nonviolent demonstrations had achieved some victories, but now these gains paled into insignificance in comparison with the goals that lay ahead. Furthermore, the opposition, except in isolated communities, was learning to blunt the effectiveness of nonviolent, legal demonstrations by protecting them and by negotiating compromises that carried as a price tag a moratorium on demonstrations. Most important, the conflict-negotiation-compromise pattern was losing its appeal to Negroes who had seen the compromises gained in negotiation result in tokenism, but who felt a growing sense of power simply because they had seen the white power structure forced to the negotiating table. The mood was increasingly one that demanded surrender to demands, not negotiation. And now the greatest response of terror and concern from white America was produced by the rioting Negro crowd. The Negro Revolution had a new cutting edge; it was violence and the threat of violence, not *Satyagraha*. No matter how dubious the incident that triggered a riot, no matter how much responsible Negro leaders condemned the violence, an outburst in any city focused attention on the long-term grievances of the ghetto residents and evoked tokens of concern from white leaders. Watts was followed by frantic activity at municipal, state, and federal levels to cope belatedly with conditions that had long existed in Los Angeles. A year later, even in the midst of talk of white backlash and of the paramount importance of law and order, the San Francisco riot of September, 1966, produced the same kind of response. The mayor appealed to the White House, not for force to suppress disorder, but for money to alleviate Negro unemployment. "I plead in the name of God and human decency for immediate emergency funds to assuage this situation," he said.[25]

Negro leaders also recognized that the threat of forceful suppression was no more a guarantee against explosion than was their own ability to negotiate with white leaders. Their recognition that a new stratum of revolutionary leadership had emerged was symbolized by the boycott of a Police Commission hearing on Negro-police relations in Los Angeles in June, 1966. Members of the United Civil Rights Council, composed of heads of major civil rights groups in the city, refused to take part in the discussion because the little-known black nationalist leaders of the Alliance of Local Organizations were not invited. The president of the local NAACP said, "The Police Commission is stupid if they do not recognize the alliance. The alliance represents hope and could prevent bloodshed and the Police Commission should recognize that fact." [26] Jerry Cohen and William S. Murphy, of *Life*, characterized the effect of the new leadership in these words, "The nationalists have one powerful effect. They force moderate leaders to take harder lines in dealing with whites. . . . The extremists, they knew, could not put over a program of their own. But they could wreck any program they didn't like." [27]

· A New Battle Cry

The battle cry that replaced "Freedom Now" during the critical years of 1965 and 1966 was not the call to arms of the Watts rioters, "Burn, Baby, Burn." It was the more enigmatic slogan, "Black Power." This cry captured the attention and the imagination of the American public during the Meredith march of the early summer of 1966. The theme, however, was not a new one. More important, those Negroes who shouted the slogan were not advocating something new; they were calling for the deliberate extension and utilization of something that already existed. For ten years, under the tutelage of the proponents of nonviolent direct action, the Negro protest movement had sought to convert white America with the power of love. White America had repeatedly responded to the power, but not to the love. Every court victory, every successful demonstration, had left a residue of feeling that the white man could be overcome, not that he could be converted. The indignant, foot-dragging and often evasive compliance of white communities with federal court orders, federal laws, and agreements accepted in biracial negotiations gave no evidence of a genuine change of heart. Faith in the fullness of the commitment even of white liberals to the Negro's welfare had steadily diminished. A century after he proclaimed it, Negro Americans were reviving Douglass' theme of power: "The law on the side of freedom is of great advantage only where there is power to make that law respected. I know of no class of my fellow-men, however just, enlightened, and humane, which can be wisely and safely trusted absolutely with the liberties of any other class." [28]

The Negro Revolution had started as a quest for freedom, and the slogan "Freedom Now" was congruent with that goal. The conviction that freedom could be gained only through power and enjoyed only when Negroes have the means in their own hands "for guarding, protecting, defending and maintaining that liberty" brought power to the forefront as the immediate goal. To dismiss the slogan "Black Power" as the wild, irrational ranting of reckless leaders seeking a place in the sun would be to deny its roots in the realities of the Negro situation in the mid-sixties.

Tokenism, encompassing all the inadequacies of Negro gains as compared to the vast needs and the rising aspirations of millions of Negroes, was a reality. Despite the perceived inadequacy of token gains, the fact that concessions had been won from white society signified that Black Power was a reality.

Evidence of this power in the political arena had existed for a long time as Negroes had shown their ability to affect the outcome of elections in key northern cities and on the national level. The election of the white liberal, Lyndon B. Johnson, had been the latest demonstration of the significance of the Negro vote as part of a liberal coalition. The most spectacular evidence of Negro political potential was to be found in a case that seemed anomalous, however, for it violated the principle of making alliances with white liberals. This was the power of Adam Clayton Powell, entrenched in the loyalties of black Harlem. Beholden to no white allies, flaunting his defiance of the white power structure before national television audiences, controlling the flow of vital legislation until he was stripped of his chairmanship and then of his seat, he demonstrated what power an unabashedly black vote could generate. Whether or not they used him as a model, Powell's existence lent a note of reality to the attempts of the Black Panther party to rally Negroes for a purely racial support of Negro candidates.

Nonviolent demonstrations and, later, riots had provided evidence of the negative power generated by social disruption. That the riots were both powerful and black was evident. The sight of Martin Luther King, Jr., leading marches day after day through white neighborhoods in Chicago in the face of massive, violent white opposition made it clear that social disruption and subsequent surrender to Negro demands, not the creation of the beloved community, was the goal even of nonviolent demonstrations. The fact that these demonstrations were sustained even while a new civil rights act hung in the balance in the Congress also signified greater reliance on Black Power. The movement was no longer attempting to mollify and reassure white allies, even in Washington. Some Negroes were declaring, "The federal government *is* the enemy!"

· The Federal Government Is the Enemy!

This declaration was to be heard in November, 1965, at a conference held in the shadow of the national capitol. It was uttered by people who were in Washington at the invitation of the President of the United States himself.

In June of the same year, one of the signs of hope and of victory for the civil rights movement was the President's announcement of his intention to call a White House conference on the fulfillment of the rights promised in the civil rights acts. The bright promise of this summit meeting of the strategists of the civil rights movement and the white liberal administration was never realized. Instead, only by skillful management of the two meetings that did result, and of the news about them, was an open, ugly break between the newly joined allies avoided. Two conferences were held, a planning conference in November and the full conference in June. While neither quite constituted a defeat or a fiasco for the Johnson administration, neither had any significant impact on the society's efforts to fulfill these rights. The conferences, particularly the one in November, did demonstrate how tenuous was the alliance between the movement and the government. It also showed how profound and pervasive was distrust of the intentions and the ability of the federal government to meet the needs of Negro Americans. These evidences of distrust of the federal government reflected an even more deep-seated mistrust of the whole American system.

In addition to the general mood of impatience with talk in lieu of action, four specific sources of disillusionment with the white Establishment destroyed the peace of the November conference. These were: (1) negative reactions to the government's posture as allegedly reflected in the famous Moynihan report; (2) chagrin at the continued impunity with which white segregationists attacked civil rights workers in the South; (3) disenchantment with the federal antipoverty program; and (4) indignation over the failure of the White House to support Commissioner of Education, Frances E. Keppel, in his showdown with the Democratic machine in Chicago.

The famous Moynihan report, *The Negro Family: The Case for National Action,* was both the stimulus for the calling of the conference and almost the cause of its cancellation.[29] This story has been told by Lee Rainwater and William Yancey.[30] They focus rather narrowly on the controversy that arose about the report and suggest that it was administrative ineptness in the political use of social science findings that led to the attack on the conference itself. Moynihan's report, prepared while he was Assistant Secretary of Labor, portrayed in forceful and deliberately selective terms how the accumulated effects of discrimination had led to the deterioration of the fabric of Negro society and of the Negro family in the ghetto. It was "critical" of the lower-class Negro family in that it presented statistics on broken families, illegitimacy, and welfare dependency. It did imply a need for self-improvement to bring lower-class Negro families in line with middle-class standards. As Rainwater and Yancey carefully document, however, the report clearly laid the blame for these conditions on discrimination; it sounded an alarm about continued Negro unemployment; and it defined the problem as one requiring federal intervention to make possible Negro self-improvement. Yet before the report had ever been seen by many of its critics, rumors and distortions originating both within and outside of government circles had made a racist monster of Daniel Patrick Moynihan. His paper was viewed by certain significant civil rights leaders as an attack on the Negro family. The White House conference was viewed as a white liberal device for evading further federal action to fulfill these rights, through an appeal for self-improvement by Negroes. In "A CORE Charge to the White House Conference," distributed in mimeographed form to participants in the November session, the radical reaction to Moynihan and the federal posture that he was alleged to symbolize was expressed in these words, "And most recently, in a new and all-embracing canard, we hear about the 'pathology of the Negro family' instead of the sickness of American society." [31]

Through skillful management, involving playing down the importance of the report, of the topic of the Negro family, and of Moynihan himself as a participant, the controversy that raged before the November conference was muted during the session. But the sensitivity of many Negro delegates to any implications of the need for self-improvement in any aspect of Negro life was evident to conference participants. Equally evident was the spirit of aggressiveness against a sick society and a white liberal government that called for more talk when more action was what was needed. Some delegates expressed the belief that the only way the conference might accomplish anything would be for the participants to embarrass the White House and thereby force the administration into vigorous action.

As significant as the Moynihan controversy was in generating dissension and distrust among the guests of the President, it must be viewed within a broader context of disillusionment.[32] While the CORE charge made only a veiled allusion to the Moynihan report, it quite explicitly criticized the Department of Justice and the operation of the American system of justice. Referring specifically to the acquittal of Thomas Coleman in Hayneville, Alabama, on charges of murdering a civil rights worker, CORE declared, "It is

a state of lawlessness and impotent government when citizens cannot be protected in the exercise of their fundamental rights. . . .
Further, a government which has laws which it cannot or will not
enforce is no government." [33]

While these declarations did not originate inside the conference,
they were reflected in one episode in which controversy did break
into the open. At the closing plenary session Clarence Mitchell, of
the NAACP, attempted to introduce a resolution, prepared by the
section on the administration of justice, calling for more vigorous
administration of federal civil rights laws. A. Philip Randolph,
who was presiding, explained that the rules of the conference, as
well as the time allotted for the session, would not permit the intro-
duction of resolutions. A stalemate of some fifteen minute's duration ensued before Mitchell relinquished the floor.

In the discussion group concerned with the community, a third
source of disenchantment with federal efforts was manifest.* The
War on Poverty was attacked in a spirit which adumbrated the
booing of Sargent Shriver some five months later. Men and
women who had worked with community action programs in the
nation's major cities reflected bitterly on the disappointments they
had experienced. Job training programs had resulted in meaning-
less make-work activities, not in employment in the private sector
of the economy. City governments had seized control of antipoverty funds and diverted significant amounts to the pockets of the
"same old city hall, white crowd." Not only had funds been way-
laid before they reached the poor, but the power that maximum
community participation was supposed to give to men who were
poor and black had also been shortstopped by politically powerful
white men.

The phrase "Black Power" was not used, but the implications of
political and economic pluralism later suggested by that slogan
were there. A woman pleaded, "Just give the poor people in the

* The author was a participant in this discussion group.

ghetto the money; they know how to organize and use it." But a sociologist objected, "No government is going to subsidize the creation of new political power; the War on Poverty is a great fraud." A Negro professional in human relations suggested that a really effective step to improve the economic status of the Negro would be for General Motors to turn over one of its divisions—Chevrolet, for example—to Negroes! A man who had been working with displaced farm workers in Mississippi proposed that the federal government should buy up idle farm land in the Delta and permit Negro cooperatives to purchase it for resettlement.

The greatest sense of betrayal by Washington seemed to stem from the suspicion that the Democratic administration was still more responsive to white political machines than it was to the Negro movement. The showdown in Chicago symbolized this. In October, Frances E. Keppel had frozen federal funds for the Chicago school system because of the adamant stand of the superintendent of schools and the mayor in the face of Negro demands for further desegregation. But within a few days Keppel released the funds, allegedly because the politically powerful mayor had secured the intervention of the White House. By the time of the November session, Keppel had resigned as commissioner and the Chicago school controversy still raged on.

It was a Negro from Chicago who declared, "The federal government is the enemy!" And it was a radical Negro leader from the same city who sounded the theme of colonialism, proposing that the federal government should establish a Department of Decolonization to deal with the problems of Negroes.

At the November planning session, an open split within the Negro protest movement and blatant defiance of the federal government were avoided, but the undercurrents of disillusionment and revolt kept the conference from fulfilling its role as a planning session. Moynihan himself observed later that the civil rights forces at this conference "managed to bring about a show of unity only in opposition to the Moynihan report, *not in effective demands on the administration.*" [34] Instead it became a preliminary hearing at which federal planners were able to detect the dangers inherent in the full conference scheduled for June. The June conference resulted in no internal crises that would enable political columnists to label it a civil rights disaster as some had the planning conference. The attempts of CORE leaders to muster opposition to the Viet Nam war failed miserably. Indeed, except for reports of this abortive effort, the conference made few headlines. The headlines of the summer of 1966 were to be captured by the newest radicals, who boycotted the conference—SNCC. By June, the split in the movement had become unmistakably evident; the undercurrents of revolution in November had become a creed for one wing of the movement. In boycotting the conference, SNCC harked back to the Moynihan controversy, by declaring, "In the process of exploiting black Americans, White America has tried to shift the responsibility for the degrading position in which blacks now find themselves away from the oppressor to the oppressed." [35]

Stokely Carmichael uttered the call to arms that he was later to shout in Mississippi: "Integration is irrelevant. Political and economic power is what the black people have to have." [36]

And a new challenge to the federal government was made part of the radical credo: "Our organization is opposed to the war in Vietnam and we cannot in good conscience meet with the chief policy maker of the Vietnam war to discuss human rights in this country when he flagrantly violates the human rights of colored people in Vietnam." [37]

· The Significance of the Conferences

When it was announced, the idea of a White House conference on civil rights seemed to symbolize the new commitment of the federal government to making race relations a major item of business. A huge federal bureaucracy concerned with a two-pronged attack on discrimination and deprivation had developed since 1964. The opinions of civil rights leaders and human relations professionals now received unprecedented attention at all levels of the federal government. The need for revolution seemed to have passed, for the President of the United States had declared that overcoming prejudice and poverty was the business of the nation, not just the concern of the demonstrators. Rainwater and Yancey interpreted both the Moynihan report and the conferences as an effort toward "the establishment of an independent federal government stance with respect to the situation of the Negro American." [38]

The disappointing reality of the conferences demonstrated the obstacles that confront a moderate government when it attempts to embrace the goals of a revolutionary movement. During the March on Washington in August, 1963, John Lewis of SNCC had desired to include in his speech the blunt question, "I want to know: which side is the Federal Government on?" [39] Lewis was persuaded by other leaders of the march to omit this passage, but the question still hung in the air. As long as the movement kept its revolutionary fervor and dreams of total victory, only one answer would be acceptable. King had made clear what this answer must be when he said, "There is a right and wrong side of this conflict and the government does not belong in the middle." [40] An essential trait of a revolutionary leader is the faith that only his definition of right is true. Right to him is the right of the crusader, not that of the practical politician nor that of the social planner. The White House conference revealed that the independent stance sought by the federal government would be one that took into account the unpleasant realities of the effects of past discrimination, as the Moynihan report did, rather than transmitting disabilities into virtues. More significant, however, was the suspicion that the most advanced position of the federal government would reflect the contemporary distribution of power, political and economic, and not the ideal redistribution of this power envisaged by Negro leaders.

Commenting further on the role of the federal government, Rainwater and Yancey proposed, "If the federal government ever actually succeeded in establishing an independent role in the civil rights area, failure to make extensive and sophisticated use of the social sciences will put the civil rights movement at a very great competitive disadvantage in bringing to bear countervailing power and proposals." [41]

There was another side to this coin, however, and the White House conference revealed it. The attempt by the federal government to put social science findings to political use shows that a moderate government that relies on an ameliorative, social engineering approach to an urgent social problem is at a competitive disadvantage with radical crusaders who seek total victory and utopian solutions. Despite the aid of the Negro vote in putting it in power, the moderate Democratic regime was still responsive to white political and economic power. It was still the government of a white man's society, and was no more willing to preside over the liquidation of white power than Winston Churchill was prepared to preside over the liquidation of the British Empire. To this extent the federal government, like state and municipal government, did reveal itself as the enemy.

· Black Power

Less than a month after the June conference the fact that the Negro Revolution had evolved a new spearhead became inescapably evident. Stokely Carmichael, who had replaced the militant John Lewis as chairman of SNCC, used the Meredith march through Mississippi as a vehicle for proclaiming "Black Power" as the newest slogan of the revolution. Neither the term nor the reality to which it referred were new. But amidst the drama of the latest confrontation of black men with the ancient enemy—southern, white, state government—with the voices of the crowd echoing the cry and the mass media broadcasting it to the world, Carmichael joined the two. No fine distinctions were made between kinds of power—political, economic; violent, nonviolent; legal, illegal; loving, hostile. The appeal was simple: let there be power which was *new* and *black*. "Black Power" was a slogan, not an ideology or a program. The response of the crowd to Carmichael did not signify that he had become the paramount leader of the Negro Revolution. It did signify that he and his imitators had introduced a new dimension into the movement. Other leaders would have to react to this new dimension, just as the NAACP had been forced to adjust to King's tactics. More significantly, the white opposition and the public would hereafter perceive the movement differently, no matter how much the older leaders sought to isolate and disarm Carmichael. Most important, the movement of the proponents of Black Power to center stage gave a new meaning to radicalism in the Negro protest movement. Howard Elinson has identified the essential distinction between the radical wing of the movement and the mainstream. He says, "We regard as radicals individuals and groups who, while supporting the cause of the Negro, dissent from any of several such traditional American values as racial equality, the restriction of social movements to legal and nonviolent means, and political change through the usual processes of representative democracy." [42]

Between 1956 and 1966 the range of tactics employed by various segments of the Negro Revolution had broadened to include all forms of coercive public protest, even violence. The newest shock troops of the revolution did not shrink from open advocacy of violence, at least as a means of self-defense, and even the most moder-

ate Negro leaders could not afford to condemn rioters in unequivocal terms. There had been a concomitant broadening of the values
of the revolution. Even when the goals of the Negro protest movement could be described simply as integration into the mainstream
of American life, white Americans had asked, "What does the
Negro want?" They had refused to accept the simple answer. Now
the answer was much more complex and incomprehensible, for the
values of the Negro Revolution had changed along with the tactics.
With this change, some of the answers to the question became not
only incomprehensible, but frightening; the movement appeared
even more revolutionary than before.

VI

Black Power:
The Revolutionary Myth

At its beginning in May, 1954, there was no place in the Negro
Revolution for dissidents who would deny the professed values of
the American democratic system. The NAACP had created a base
of power to effect changes in the practices of society. It had done
so, however, through skillful use of the white man's law. All that
was asked was to make the application of the traditional values of
the American system color-blind, not to change these values. The
Communist party was caught flat-footed by the success of the
NAACP in the school desegregation cases. It was still telling Negro
Americans that there was no hope for them in a capitalist society
in which they were an exploited nation. Black nationalism of the
Muslim variety was an anachronistic hangover from the days of
Marcus Garvey. To suspect that the Negro protest movement
sought anything other than what white people wanted was the
mark of the paranoid segregationist. The Negro simply wanted to
enter the mainstream of American life.

· The Changing Values of the Revolution

During the years since the beginning of the revolution, the crystal
clarity of the values has given way to confusion. How confused and

diverse the values had become by 1966 is revealed by a letter from a Negro leader in Los Angeles. James H. Hargett spoke to the people of the city through a letter to the Los Angeles *Times*.[1] The letter read as follows:

The indictments of Negro Leadership on the part of John McCone made it absolutely essential that I address myself to his seeming obsession on the question of Negro leadership.

There is one thing the Negro community shares with almost every other ethnic group in its efforts to solve its problems and give direction to the basic aspirations of its people. They are three dominant ideas.

The first idea is one of complete separation. This simply means the conviction that the Negro community would be better off if its white exploiters would leave or be driven out to permit self determination to express itself economically, socially, educationally, and religiously.

The second idea is one of complete integration. This idea is best described in the speech of Dr. Martin Luther King at the famous March on Washington, which is best known by his words "I had a dream." In this dream Dr. King spoke of little black boys and little white boys, little black girls and little white girls, and all the rest of America living harmoniously in a totally integrated society.

The third idea is the affirmation of America being a pluralistic society and an acceptance of the fact that the Negro American, like the Jew, will never be fully accepted into the mainstream of American society. Therefore, the drive should be towards instilling pride in Negro equality, developing the highest possible education and skills, broadening and deepening cultural appreciations and artistic endeavors all in the interest of strengthening the group but never pursuing the evasive dream of unconditional integration.

Each one of these ideas has an articulate leader or leaders in the Negro community with a significant following. So far, these three ideas have experienced a kind of peaceful co-existence with the ever present possibility that one of the

three might make a power grab and thus initiate the "fratri-
cidal phase" of the Negro Revolution.

I suspect that the traditional leadership image of the Negro
whose primary value to the white community was his ability
to keep down trouble that in any form or fashion inconven-
ienced the white community, no longer exists.

The real issue before us is which of the three expressed
ideological points of view will emerge with the predominant
power. With the other possibility being of the continuation of
all three with almost equal power which will force them to
peacefully co-exist. Such an outcome will complicate things
for the white power structure for it will have to relate to all
three of them in the search for consensus on certain policies,
practices, political leadership and many other concerns.

The contrast between the complicated situation portrayed by
Hargett and the clarity of goals of the early days of the movement
is sharpened by the observation of Pat Watters, a member of the
staff of the Southern Regional Council. Watters said of the early
days, "It used to be so wonderfully simple, here were these Negroes
and they were right. There were those segregated lunch counters.
In an age of ambivalence, of moral ambiguity, the Negro movement gave us, at last, a choice, as clear cut as a sit-in, between good
and evil." [2]

For the values of a social movement to change is not unusual. No
matter how clear the vision of the holy grail is at the inception of
the movement, the storm clouds of internal controversy and external opposition distort this vision as the movement progresses
through its career. Characteristically there is a broadening and an
elaboration of the values to include a larger number of specific
goals and demands. Movements start with very limited and specific goals, but frequently end with almost global programs that demand a total reform of the society. During this process, vagueness
and inconsistency in the specific goals may develop so that the total
program becomes very diffuse and often contains contradictory

propositions. It is this sort of process that Harold Isaacs has described when he says of the Negro movement, "The goal of integration, like freedom for the anti-colonialists stands like a great shining blur down at the far end of the struggle road, drawing and inspiring all who fight for it, but becoming not clearer, but blurrier, the closer one gets to it." [3]

· Power as a Goal

As blurry as the goals may be, the longer the struggle to achieve them continues the greater and greater is the preoccupation with the overriding goal of victory. Victory comes to mean achieving a position of power that will enable the members of the movement to work out their own destiny. The original goals become ultimate and, therefore, remote objectives. Consideration of the practical details and how they are to be implemented is deferred, supposedly until after the victory. The immediate objective becomes achieving sufficient power to permit the proponents of the ultimate objectives to work out their program without interference by the opponents of the movement. It is a commonplace of history that very often when revolutions do succeed in gaining power, the values with which they started get lost. In this manner the most idealistic value-oriented movement can become power-oriented. The power orientations of the Negro movement have been steadily increasing, as has been pointed out. Hence, the Black Power advocates represent the vanguard of the movement, not merely the lunatic fringe, as they are so often portrayed.

· Why Black Power?

It is not difficult to envisage the reasons for the rise of the vision symbolized by the slogan "Black Power." Samuel Dubois Cook suggests two reasons:

First there is the experience of bitter disappointment, disgust, and despair over the pace, scope and quality of social change. . . . A second source of the myth of Black Power was the prolonged and direct encounter of certain civil rights workers—especially those connected with SNCC and CORE—with the grim and aching realities, the dark and brute actions and deceptions of certain sections of the Deep South.[4]

Ironically, the bitter disappointment of which Cook speaks arose not just from the adamancy of the resistance, but also from the experiences of Negroes in working with white allies. This helps to explain why the power the movement seeks came to be labeled Black Power. Even in the inner circles of SNCC and CORE the harsh reality that America is a white man's society intruded. Thus in the words of a young, white civil rights worker, Bruce Detwiler, there arose "a time to be black." Detwiler wrote, "Since the organizer's purpose is not to lead, but to get the people to lead themselves, being white is an insurmountable handicap. After a while organizers often wonder if they are not unwittingly developing a new breed of Uncle Tom, to put it harshly—a Tom who will do and think whatever the white civil rights worker wants him to." [5]

This is not to say that the new radicals have won control of the movement. There is no large, clearly defined following to whom Stokely Carmichael or his successor H. Rap Brown can appeal. SNCC is the smallest and most loosely structured of the major protest organizations. Floyd McKissick of CORE echoes Carmichael's theme, but how many of CORE's members subscribe to the philosophy of Black Power is undetermined. Certainly the leaders of the larger organizations, the NAACP, SCLC, and the National Urban League, as well as the patriarch of the movement, A. Philip Randolph, have renounced the slogan in vigorous terms. Yet as Cook says of the slogan, "It makes crowds roar, conversations sparkle, and the television cameras click. It wins headlines. After all it made Stokely Carmichael a national figure over night." [6]

• The White Reaction

Even more important is the reaction of white Americans to the strident voices of the Black Power advocates. The bitter division within the Negro protest movement that was revealed by the confrontation between Stokely Carmichael and Martin Luther King during the Meredith march was conveniently overlooked or forgotten by many white Americans, particularly those opposed to any further extension of Negro rights. Particularly when set against the background of riots in Los Angeles and other cities, Carmichael's inflammatory words were perceived as ample evidence that civil rights demonstrations were getting completely out of hand. That King was still pleading desperately for adherence to nonviolent tactics; that far more violence had been initiated by white counter-demonstrators than by Negro demonstrators; that of thirty-four people killed in the Watts riots, thirty-one were Negro (and in Detroit, thirty-four of forty-two were Negro); were all conveniently overlooked. The Harris polls conducted in the fall of 1966 showed a dramatic rise in the percentage of white respondents who felt that Negroes were trying to go too fast in their demands for change and in the proportion who disapproved of the methods used by civil rights advocates. The public definition of the Negro protest movement as revolutionary was becoming even stronger.

• The White Backlash: So-called or Real?

This public definition reflects the white backlash. Yet many liberal observers speak of the "so-called" white backlash, implicitly denying the reality of this much-discussed phenomenon. The reasons for this reluctance to accept the reality of a significant growth in white resistance to the Negro Revolution may be easily identified.

Opponents of the revolution are eager to point to the backlash as conclusive evidence that the movement has become self-defeating. They no longer need to seek moral justification for their opposition to militant tactics and the goals toward which these tactics are directed. With a great pretense of objectivity, and even a sympathy for the Negro, they can simply say, "Let's look at the facts." The liberal does not want to accept the fact of the white backlash because he does not want to fall into the trap thus set by the resistance.

In addition, to face squarely the reality and significance of both Black Power and the white backlash would be to accept the fact of the polarization of race relations and the applicability of a conflict model for interpreting them. This does great violence to liberal optimism that assumes that "the integrative effects of consensus about the American Creed as well as the cohesive qualities of the American social system will limit the destructiveness of the explosion triggered by the collision of white and Negro interest." [7]

An example of this kind of reluctance to accept the white backlash as a reality is found in an analysis of the victories of Mrs. Louise Day Hicks, chairman of the Boston School Committee, by J. Michael Ross, Thomas Crawford, and Thomas Pettigrew.[8] They attempted to answer the question, "Is there a 'white backlash'?" by analysis of attitudinal data collected in Boston, as well as the results of surveys by the National Opinion Research Center. They concluded: "The much touted 'white backlash,' the white counterattack to Negro civil rights activities, though much prophesied during the George Wallace and Barry Goldwater ascendancies, never materialized for Goldwater and has never been confirmed by social science research." [9]

They find evidence for this conclusion in the fact of steadily increasing white support for the *goals* of the civil rights movement. But they go on to say, "As in our Boston data, there were negative sentiments expressed about the *means* of achieving racial change, but this was nothing new. Such sentiments are expressed by many white Americans each time a new protest technique—sit-ins, freedom rides, street demonstrations—is introduced." [10]

But there *is* the reality of the white backlash. It is the newest version of the American dilemma. There has come to exist a new and popular acceptance of equality of opportunity for qualified Negroes. This is the modern, more enlightened application of the general valuations of the American creed to include the Negro literally as a member of the class of "all men" who, according to the Declaration of Independence, were created "equal." The white backlash consists of a reluctance to accept those *intermediate* steps that are necessary to make equality a reality for the many Negroes who are in no way prepared to live according to white middle-class standards. Desegregation has become respectable, or at least has been accepted as inevitable, in all parts of the land except the most recalcitrant sections of the Deep South. But the desegregation that has become respectable is token. It will continue to be so because of the sophistication of white people as to means of evading total integration, as well as the economic and educational incapacity of most Negroes to overcome the formally color-blind barriers to upward mobility. Certainly no later than a few days after the Los Angeles riot, it became inescapably clear that gradual and token integration was no longer acceptable to the Negro masses, nor to any but the most conservative Negroes.

David Danzig has described this shift from the civil rights movement to the Negro Revolution in these words:

> What we have here, in effect, is a radical departure from the traditional conception of civil rights as the rights of individuals. This departure lies at the heart of the "Negro Revolution" and may, indeed, almost be said to be that revolution. . . . What is now perceived as the revolt of the Negro amounts to this; the solitary Negro seeking admission into the white world through unusual achievement has been re-

placed by the organized Negro insisting upon a legitimate share for his group of the goods of American Society. The white liberal, in turn, who—whether or not he has been fully conscious of it—has generally conceived of progress in race relations as the one-by-one assimilation of deserving Negroes into the larger society, finds himself confused and threatened by suddenly having to come to terms with an aggressive Negro community that wishes to enter it *en masse*.[11]

· **The Real Backlash**

It is the immediate steps necessary to make possible this entrance of the Negro community into society *en masse* that an increasing number of white people show themselves reluctant to accept. It is preferential treatment of Negroes in hiring practices in order to counterbalance the effect of years of discrimination. It is radical revision of patterns of school attendance to overcome the built-in tokenism maintained by the cherished neighborhood school and the homogeneous neighborhood. And the research of Ross, Crawford, and Pettigrew itself indicates strongly that "behind the resistance to school desegregation lies the greater fear of neighborhood desegregation; and even beyond that fear that the good old ways of life will change as Negroes move in." [12]

But the white people who are now resisting the movement are not the ancient foe, the southern whites. They are Jews, traditional liberal friends of Negroes, now defending their middle-class suburban neighborhoods and their neighborhood schools.[13] They are Americans of Irish, Italian, or Polish descent defending their labor unions, their neighborhood schools, and the imagined integrity of their neighborhoods. A labor leader said of these people, "a lot of blue-collar workers are first and second generation in this country and to them those nasty brick bungalows are almost holy." [14] And there are, finally, the old American Protestants as well.

As Danzig has pointed out, this does not mean that white people outside the South are becoming racist in the old tradition of southern white supremacy. As he says:

> Often they are merely a more coherent and readily identifiable segment of the working and middle-class urban population which may embrace integration as a plank in the democratic platform, but which is becoming militantly separatist at the local level where it lives under the heavy pressure of an expanding Negro population. The attempt of Negroes to penetrate adjacent white minority group neighborhoods not only arouses personal prejudice and individual defensiveness; it also arouses the fear that the cherished neighborhood culture will be destroyed.[15]

To put it very simply, an increasing number of white Americans will assent to the proposition that Negroes should share more fully, even equally, in the good things of American life. At the same time an increasing number are demonstrating that they are unwilling to give up any part of their share of these good things in order to provide equality for the Negro. On the local level these good things are schools that have not reached the tipping point; union locals toward which the members have a proprietary attitude; and neighborhoods that it is hoped will remain stable rather than undergoing transition and inundation by Negroes. On the national level, the matter is almost as simple as the tax dollar versus the welfare dollar. As the Viet Nam conflict drags on, it is also becoming an issue of guns versus butter. The "haves" of an affluent society are willing for the "have-nots" to gain only so long as it is not at their expense. These "haves" are not simply so many discrete, unrelated individuals, however. In the words of Nathan Glazer:

> The white community into which the Negro now demands full entrance is not actually a single community—it is a series of communities. And all of them feel threatened by the

implications of the new Negro demand for full equality. . . .
The Negro now demands entry into a world, a society that
does not exist except in ideology. In that world there is only
one American community, and in that world, heritage, ethnicity, religion, race are only incidental and accidental personal characteristics.[16]

· Black Pluralism

After a long and partially successful battle against the monolith of
southern white resistance, the Negro has encountered a new, multi-
faceted resistance outside the South, arising partly out of the pluralism of white America. To this resistance one wing of the Negro
movement has responded with a pluralism of its own. Even while
the NAACP, at first, and CORE and SCLC, later, were giving the
Negro protest movement an exclusively assimilationist theme, there
was a glacial sort of pluralism among the Negro masses. While
they applauded the prophets of integration from afar and sometimes followed them into the streets, thousands of Negroes continued to support the segregated institutions of the enduring Negro
community. One of the major points of controversy in many local
communities, between the liberals of the black bourgeoisie and the
seemingly conservative poor Negroes, has been whether new but
segregated institutions should be built, however great the need.
Even after the militance of the Watts riot, a controversy raged
between Negroes in the city of Los Angeles over the plea of some
Watts residents for the construction of a junior college in the
ghetto.

As disillusionment with the results of ten years of militant assim-
ilationism set in, voices appeared in the Negro community advocating pluralism as a goal to be sought, not an unfortunate condition
to be accepted only so long as necessary. New forms of black nationalism not burdened by the exotic religious ideology and the

separatism of the Black Muslims began to appear. The open expression of hostility to Whitey by Negroes became commonplace. Supplementing the new black nationalism was what might be called colored anticolonialism, which linked the new radicals of the Negro Revolution with the new anarchists of the student movement. Both reflected the theme that white society and, specifically, an American society that was prosecuting the war against colored men in Viet Nam, were sick and defunct. A corollary of this theme was the denial that there was any hope of aid from the Establishment. To the new radicals of the Negro Revolution the Establishment was now a white liberal Establishment. The President of the United States himself became the foremost symbol of the moral bankruptcy of white liberalism. The values cherished by middle-class whites, including liberals, also lost their luster. Rather than wanting to enter the mainstream of American society, the new radicals called for a drastic diversion of that mainstream.

· A New Variety of Pluralism

The pluralism of Negro Americans should not be confused with the historic pluralism of other American ethnic groups. It is a pluralism formed of frustration and disillusionment, not of hope and a long-established sense of peoplehood. Negroes do not have the pride in an ancient religion and the loyalty to a people who have suffered for this religion for centuries that the Jews possess. They do not have the identification with a nationality that has struggled for years or even centuries to achieve nationhood that gave the Italians, the Poles, and the Irish a ready-made identity and a fierce pride even as they sought political freedom and economic opportunity in a tolerant America. They do not even have the pride in *la raza y la gente* that has enabled Mexican-Americans to hold their heads high in the face of prejudice and discrimination. Removed by thousands of miles and three centuries from a homeland that they long since ceased to claim, Negro Americans lack even the sense of identity that characterizes the "Island centered community" of Puerto Ricans in New York.[17] Their religion tells them to worship a white God. Their cultural history stretches back only to the degradation of slavery, not to the glories of ancient African empires. In the struggle of the new nonwhite nations to achieve nationhood, Negro Americans see a corollary to their own colonial plight, not a black counterpart of *eretz Israel.* The successes of the new nations of Africa are as much a source of shame as of pride to Negro Americans because of their own failure to achieve freedom now. To put it bluntly, Negro Americans find little in their history as a people of which to be proud; pride must be in the future. As has been so often observed in recent years, Negro Americans are searching for an identity. L. Singer has observed that Negroes are just in the process of becoming an ethnic group after a long period of being a collection of unrelated individuals "without the community of tradition, sentiment and so forth that has marked other populations and given rise to ethnic groups such as the Italian Immigrants." [18] Singer observes further:

> As the Negroes become more an ethnic group—more focused and organized—it may be expected that rather than reacting to the actions of white [sic], they will increasingly act along paths of action chosen to achieve their goal of full, individual participation in the larger society. It can be added that any successes can be expected to pave the way for increased activity. It may be further hypothesized that as the barriers to full participation yield and slowly crumble, frustration and impatience over the differences between actuality and aspirations may prompt segments of the Negro group to manifest radical and separatist (anti-white) sentiments such as the "black Muslim movement." It is doubtful that any of these organizations will be large. Size, however, should not

be confused with importance. By defining one end of the spectrum of Negro responses, such groups will affect the thinking of all Negroes. Further, because of the impact upon the whites, they may contribute to the general struggle for Negro aspirations despite their separatist orientations.[19]

· Black Power as Myth

Singer's words, written in 1962, were indeed prophetic. "Black Power" has arisen as a slogan that symbolizes the emerging pluralism and ethnicity of Negro Americans. It suggests a way in which pride, not to be found in the past, may be created in the future. Furthermore, Black Power has become the myth of the Negro Revolution, replacing the earlier myth, freedom now. It is the kind of myth of which the French syndicalist, Georges Sorel spoke when he wrote:

> Experience shows that the *framing of the future, in some indeterminate time*, may, when it is done in a certain way, be very effective, and have very few inconveniences; this happens when the anticipations of the future take the form of those myths, which enclose with them, all the strongest inclinations of the people, of a party or of a class, inclinations which recur to the mind with the insistence of instincts in all the circumstances of life; and which give an aspect of complete reality to the hopes of immediate action by which, more easily than by any other method, men can reform their desires, passions, and mental activity. . . . The myth must be judged as a means of acting on the present; any attempt to discuss how far it can be taken literally as future history is devoid of sense.[20]

Those rational, eminently practical observers who, with such confidence, denounce Black Power as the tragic fantasy of the lunatic fringe would do well to remember Browning's words, "If a

man's reach does not exceed his grasp, then what's a heaven for?"
Ironically, the Black Power proponents call for Negroes to do
many of the same things that white people have criticized them for
not doing. Thus Stokely Carmichael says, "If we are to proceed
toward true liberation, we must cut ourselves off from white people. We must form our own institutions, credit unions, co-ops, political parties, write our own histories. . . . The charge may be
made that we are 'racists,' but whites who are sensitive to our
problems will realize that we must determine our own destiny." [21]

There is no objective or logical evidence that Negroes can create
a viable parallel economy within the economic framework of the
United States. Nor is it likely that they can create a black government even in the minority of counties in which Negroes are poten-
tially the majority of the electorate. At the same time, any significant gain in Negro economic and political power will enhance the
bargaining position of the Negro community.

This is not to imply, however, that Black Power is simply a vision of cultural pluralism. Nor is it to suggest that Stokely Carmichael regards it as a myth, as a vision that is not literally attaina-
ble. Carmichael points to another aspect of the issue when he says:

> The need for psychological equality is the reason why
> SNCC today believes that blacks must organize in the black
> community. Only black people can convey the revolutionary
> idea that black people are able to do things themselves. Only
> they can help create in the community an aroused and con-
> tinuing black consciousness that will provide the basis for
> political strength.[22]

It is the demand for psychological equality and political power
that frightens so many white people, and which causes Black
Power to be equated with black violence and even black supremacy. Here the confusion in the goals of the Negro Revolution gen-

erates a confused and frightened white reaction. While Stokely
Carmichael declaims of Black Power, Martin Luther King, Jr.,
leads marches demanding that white neighborhoods be opened for
Negro occupancy. While the new radicals of the Negro movement
talk about getting the white colonial occupation forces out of the
Negro community, the earlier generation of Negro leaders still
talks about getting Negroes into white neighborhoods, white
schools, and white factories. While King talks about the power of
nonviolent confrontation, Carmichael says, "As for initiating the
use of violence, we hope that such programs as ours will make that
unnecessary; but it is not for us to tell black communities whether
they can or cannot use any particular form of action to resolve
their problems." [23] H. Rap Brown cries, "If America don't come
around, we're going to burn America down." Many white people
respond to these confused signals by envisioning a society consist-
ing not of proud, self-sufficient Negroes living in their own ethnic
enclaves, but of thousands of dirty, lawless, uneducated, vice-
ridden Negroes swarming out of the ghettoes into white neighborhoods. As Carmichael puts it, "To most whites, Black Power seems
to mean that the Mau Mau are coming to the suburbs at night." [24]
Those Negro leaders who try to drown the theme of Black Power
by shouting over and over, "Freedom Now" and "Nonviolence"
are not only fighting a losing battle, they are also contributing to
the growth of white fears and the backlash which will make the appeal of Black Power even greater to Negroes.

Whatever nightmare visions of black supremacy they may have
conjured up, the Black Power advocates, with their indubitably
socialist orientation, have done what the previous generation of
militant Negro leadership seemed incapable of doing. They have
given their wholehearted support to the needs of the hard core of
unassimilable Negroes without a backward glance at what this may
do to the aspirations of the black bourgeoisie. The history of the

tactics of love show clearly that while these tactics produce temporary feelings of pride and the illusion of victory, they also produce a hangover of frustration at the tokenism and broken agreements that have so often followed. David Danzig says of the Negro movement and Black Power:

> Though one cannot speak of the Negro movement as though it were monolithic and had clearly defined priorities and goals, one might describe its broad aspirations as directed toward "the good life." . . . But if the Negro movement can be said to be centered on material welfare it has a redemptive side as well; it seeks a rediscovery of pride and confidence and it couples communal self-assertion with individual self respect.[25]

Black Power, the first slogan to emphasize this idea of communal self-assertion, originally shocked white ears in the South. Yet it is essentially a northern product, having as it does a particularly profound meaning on the home ground of the liberal coalitions, in the cities where Negro expectations have escalated. In the ghettoes, the welfare goal has much higher salience in comparison to the status goal of integration than it does in the traditionally segregated South.

The emphasis of the new radicals of SNCC has not been limited to welfare goals, of course, nor has SNCC been the only organization emphasizing these goals. At the other end of the spectrum of militancy stands the National Urban League. For years it has endured the taunts of other organizations for emphasizing welfare and Negro self-improvement rather than integration. Whitney Young's Domestic Marshall Plan spells out the details of a radical revision of the economic structure. But SNCC is not the Urban League in dirty dungarees. Whitney Young has been an unofficial advisor to presidents; Stokely Carmichael calls the President of the United States a warmonger. The Urban League gains white support by warning that the "fire next time" will come if its program is not implemented. SNCC leaves the impression that it is ready to light the fire.

• The Road to Black Power

Hence, the totality of the myth of Black Power must be considered, not just the economic, political, and social pluralism that it implies. First of all, the theme of Black Power as elaborated by its prophet Stokely Carmichael calls for a socialist America. Hear Carmichael's words:

> In Lowndes County 86 white families owned 90 percent of the land. What are black people in that county going to do for jobs; where are they going to get money? There must be reallocation of land, of money. Ultimately the economic foundations of this country must be shaken if black people are to control their lives.
>
> For racism to die a totally different America must be born. . . . The society we seek to build among black people, then, is not a capitalist one. It is a society in which the spirit of community and humanistic love prevail.[26]

When the new radicals speak, as they rarely do, of coalitions with white people, they do not have in mind coalitions with white liberals who wish to redeem the white man's society by making a place in it for the well-scrubbed, well-educated, "qualified" Negro. While Carmichael tells white civil rights workers that they are not wanted in SNCC, he does not mean that there is no place for them in the Negro Revolution. He makes their place quite explicit when he says, "It is purely academic today to talk about bringing poor blacks and whites together, but the job of creating a poor white power block must be attempted. The main responsibility for it falls upon whites."[27]

But the new radicals go farther than the Urban League or any other of the relatively moderate protest groups in rejecting the American system as it is. Not only do they reject the economic system, the existing political alignments, and the bourgeois values of America; they also reject the nationalism of late twentieth century America. The alliance of the radical wing of the Negro protest movement with the anti-Viet Nam war movement reflects the intrusion of the Third World theme into the ideology of the Negro Revolution. The Third World encompasses those peoples who are distinguished from the major powers not by their allegiance to capitalism or communism, but by being the victims of colonialism. In addressing themselves to poor Negroes and castigating the black bourgeoisie, the new radicals implicitly align the Negro movement with this Third World. In summarizing the areas of agreement between the various elements of the new radicalism, Howard Elinson observes:

> First, all share the view that American society is basically unsatisfactory and in need of changes too extreme to be brought about by gradual reforms. Second, they view the mainstream groups—King's SCLC, NAACP, liberal Democrats, etc.—as part of the Establishment or tools of the Establishment, who while pretending to work for change, are really helping to preserve the status quo. Finally, they agree that changes in the underdeveloped world are of great relevance to the American Negro. They believe that the struggle of the American Negro is not an isolated movement in American history, but, rather, is part of the broader worldwide struggle of the oppressed or nonwhite or colonial peoples.[28]

When Floyd McKissick denounces American participation in Viet Nam, and Stokely Carmichael labels Negro soldiers fighting there "mercenaries," they are reflecting more than a personal pacifism or a disloyalty born of despair. They are, instead, reflecting an inchoate faith in a new wave of the future. Despite the apparently overwhelming forces arrayed against the Impossible Revolution domestically, the hope remains that allies can be found abroad as the emerging nations of Africa and Asia and the revolutionary parties of Latin America grow stronger. The apparent inability of American military might to crush the Viet Cong and their Hanoi supporters lends credence to this hope. For the United States to leave the field to the nonwhite guerrillas would make the domestic Impossible Revolution appear a little more plausible. Carmichael reveals his faith in the Third World when he says:

> The colonies of the United States—and this includes the black ghetto within its borders, North and South—must be liberated. For a century this nation has been like an octopus of exploitation, its tentacles stretching from Mississippi and Harlem to South America, the Middle East, Southern Africa, and Viet Nam. The form of exploitation varies from area to area but the essential result has been the same—a powerful few has been maintained and enriched at the expense of the poor and voiceless colored masses. This pattern must be broken. As its grip loosens here and there around the world, the hopes of Black Americans become more realistic. For racism to die a totally different America must be born.[29]

Finally, arousing the greatest fear and righteous indignation among white Americans are the overtones of violence that distinguish the theme of the new radicals from the message of their militant rivals, such as SCLC. At one end of the spectrum is the justification for retaliatory violence manifest in the existence of the Deacons for Defense and Justice and sanctioned by the traditionally nonviolent CORE under the new leadership of Floyd McKissick. At the other end is the expatriate Robert F. Williams advocating a strategy of guerrilla warfare and sabotage in the major metropolitan centers where Negroes are concentrated. Every time a Negro throws a Molotov cocktail in a Negro ghetto, every time the National Guard must be called in to put down a riot, the credibility of Williams' appeal increases. During the summer of 1967, Stokely Carmichael moved to a position identical to that of Williams. Both he and his successor, H. Rap Brown, conjure up the vision of a Williams-style insurrection if Black Power is pushed to its ultimate form. Carmichael rejects exclusive reliance on tactics of non-violence when he says, "Wherever the honkies got injustice, we're going to tear their cities apart." [30]

· The Choice for Negro Americans

Thus there has developed in the Negro protest movement a factional division, and the course of the movement hangs in the balance. On the one hand, there is the strategy of nonviolence, of negotiation, of practical attempts to create coalitions with white Americans deemed not beyond redemption, but capable of being brought to recognize the true meaning of traditional American values. On the other hand, there is the go-for-broke strategy that rests on the faith that there will be a new America in a new world in which racism will have been destroyed not by love but by fear of the power of colored revolutionaries. It is between these strategies that Negro Americans will choose in the years ahead.

To argue to the new revolutionaries that their dream is an impossible one is as fruitless as it would have been to urge George Washington to give up the struggle during the dark days at Valley Forge. Revolutionaries have never been "summer soldiers"; it is faith, not assurance of victory, that sustains them. Moreover, the new radicals can look to more recent examples to sustain their belief that not even the power of modern centralized governments makes the revolution of the seemingly powerless irrelevant in to-day's world. They can and do point to the victory of Castro and to the long and yet inconclusive struggle of the Viet Cong. They can even point to the failure of inability of the federal government to repress white violence in the South.

That the new radicals can find ample evidence to sustain their belief that the Impossible Revolution can rebuild America in the image they desire does not mean that their faith is justified. Whether they will gain enough support among Negro Americans to make the effort depends in part upon the reactions of white society to the latest phase of the crisis in race relations. It will depend also on events abroad and their repercussions on the home front. Finally there remains the ominous question, "Will the brave dreams of the revolutionaries end in a nightmare of violent repression in a new, fascist America that neither black radicals nor white liberals desire or even envision?"

VII

The Negro Revolution: Possible or Impossible?

From May 17, 1954 until the March on Washington and the passage of the 1964 Civil Rights Act, the battle over segregation forcibly reminded the American people that race relations constituted their foremost domestic problem. Just as the end of this battle seemed to be at hand, it became evident that there existed a crisis that was far graver than the desegregation controversy had ever been.

Fantastic gains had been made in terms of judicial interpretation of the Constitution, of federal legislation, and of public acceptance of the "qualified" Negroes of the black bourgeoisie. The federal antipoverty program represented a broad attack on the plight of the poor, white as well as nonwhite, not originally envisioned as part of the war on inequality. With the death of the doctrine of separate but equal, the nation had a new, albeit incomplete, commitment to an equality of opportunity that was color blind.

• Integration: A Fading Goal

Now it appeared, however, that integration had lost its luster as a goal. In practice it had turned out to mean the token integration of a minority of qualified Negroes into what remained a white man's society. For the majority of Negro Americans, handicapped by generations of isolation from the mainstream of American culture, the mere relaxing of racial barriers could not mean "Freedom Now." In acknowledgment of this new facet of the Negro's problem, Whitney Young called for "a decade of dedicated special effort" to close the gap created by three hundred years of preferential treatment of white citizens. He said, "At this point when the scales of justice are so grossly unbalanced it is impossible to balance them by simply applying equal weight." [1] James Farmer, militant leader of CORE, soon to be replaced by the even more militant Floyd McKissick, expressed the same theme in stronger terms. He said of the impoverished Negro, "Offering him equal rights, even equal opportunity at this late date without giving him a special boost is the kind of cruel joke American individualism has played on the poor throughout history. And so CORE and the Movement of which we are part planned compensatory and remedial programs to provide the necessary boost." [2]

· The New Crisis

The new crisis in race relations arose from this basic fact: an emergency program giving Negroes preferential treatment on the basis of their color, not just the mere cessation of crude color discrimination, was necessary to make equality meaningful for Negroes. Two years of experience with seemingly radical civil rights laws and with the much-vaunted War on Poverty revealed that both attempts fell far short of the kind of special effort that was needed. The near-rebellion of Negro leaders at the White House planning conference and the ghetto riots in the summers of 1965, 1966, and 1967 symbolized how far a decade of favorable court rulings, nonviolent demonstrations, and federal legislation had fallen short of satisfying the rising expectations of the Negro masses. It was evident that the Negro protest movement was at a critical juncture. To continue to pick away at segregation, the symbol of the Negro's inferior social and economic position, was not enough. An assault on the *de facto* inequality of the Negro masses in employment, housing, and education was now mandatory. The tactics of protest that had been effective in desegregating lunch counters and parks and in producing federal legislation were being brought into question.

· A New "New Deal"

First, there was a widespread fear even among militant Negro leaders that the limits of reform through federal civil rights laws had been reached. Effective enforcement of existing laws, a spirit of compliance on the local level, and broader social legislation were now needed. The failure of Congress to pass the 1966 civil rights bill suggested that this law-making body, too, felt that there were enough civil rights laws on the books. There was also an obvious fear among civil rights leaders that demonstrations could no longer be disciplined and nonviolent. The riots of the summers of 1965, 1966, and 1967 had revealed to Negro leaders how little control they had over the inhabitants of the ghettoes. This apprehension led to another fear that continuation of the strategy of protest would alienate significant white support of the Negro movement and lead to a pervasive and clear-cut definition of the movement as revolutionary.

Bayard Rustin, whose credentials as a militant leader were impeccable, stated the case for a new strategy and new tactics in his famous article entitled "From Protest to Politics; the Future of the Civil Rights Movement." The strategy that Rustin suggested was radical, for he called for a shift from civil rights as a target to a program of "qualitative transformation of fundamental institutions, more or less rapidly, to the point where the social and economic structure which they comprised can no longer be said to be the same." [3] In amplification he called for "radical programs for full employment, abolition of slums, the reconstruction of our educational system, new definitions of work and leisure. . . . Adding up the cost of such programs we can only conclude that we are talking about a refashioning of our political economy." [4] He suggested that the civil rights movement had run its course and would have to be replaced by a broader social movement devoted to economic and political reform. There should be, in effect, a new New Deal and an enlargement of the Great Society to gargantuan proportions.

Rustin's proposal for bringing about these reforms was also reminiscent of the early days of Roosevelt's New Deal. Reflecting an optimism generated by the democratic sweep in the elections of 1964 he said:

> The future of the Negro struggle depends on whether the contradictions of this society can be resolved by a coalition of progressive forces which becomes the effective political majority in the United States. I speak of the coalition which staged the March on Washington, passed the Civil Rights Act and laid the basis for the Johnson landslide: Negroes, trade unionists, liberals and religious groups.[5]

It was in the same vein that, a few months later, A. Philip Randolph called for a one hundred and eighty-five billion dollar Freedom Budget to make possible full equality for Negroes. Randolph made it plain that he believed only a comprehensive, far-reaching federal program could accomplish the job. Both Rustin and Randolph emphasized the benefits that would accrue to the entire economy if Negro poverty were abolished and, along with it, the poverty of all deprived Americans.

Such a solution as Rustin and Randolph proposed would indeed provide an unprecedented model of peaceful social change as an alternative to revolution. The dream of the New Deal, revived as the vision of the Great Society, would become reality as poverty, poor housing, and inferior schools were abolished for all Americans. In the process of achieving this reality, race consciousness would also be abolished as ambitious, upwardly mobile whites and Negroes made common cause against the ancient, impersonal evils of poverty, disease, and ignorance. A utopian society would be created without the ordeal of either a class war or a race war, but through a marvel of social engineering.

· Guns or Butter: A Problem of Values

Nowhere is there evidence, however, that the majority of the American electorate is disposed to pay the price for such a feat. That the price would be small as compared to the cost of Viet Nam or the space program does not change the fact that the American public is willing to pay for these latter ventures, but not for the former. The affluence of the majority of the population accounts in part for this phenomenon. In the words of two sociologists Sidney Wilhelm and Elwin Powell: "Our society prospers without a redistribution of income in favor of the lower brackets—despite liberal slogans. In the military system we have an impersonal, omnipotent consumer of tremendous proportions that, in effect, supplants a mass purchasing power that could have been placed in the Negro's hands." [6]

Economists and sociologists who take a pessimistic view of the crisis of automation predict that the problems of "uselessness" that now confront the Negro masses will eventually be recognized as a problem of whites also. Wilhelm and Powell comment, "For the Negro is merely a weathervane for the future. *His* experience will be a common one for many whites now deprived of some sort of usefulness; *his* frustrations will become those for many others the longer we hesitate to confront the meaning of human dignity in an automated society." [7]

The time in which the anxiety of the Negro is generalized to a large segment of potential political allies in white society has not yet arrived. The congressional and gubernatorial elections of November 1966, showed the existence of a backlash against the welfare programs of the Great Society, not a readiness to expand these programs. At a time when a radical program of social and economic reform was needed, the American people opted for moderation. Daniel Moynihan observed after these elections, "It appears that the nation may be in the process of reproducing the tragic events of the Reconstruction: giving to Negroes the forms of legal equality but withdrawing the economic and political resources which are the bases of social equality." [8]

In the meantime, the urgent needs and the intense dissatisfaction of the aroused Negro masses remained a present fact. The Negro Revolution had to continue in some fashion unless race relations were to enter a new era of accommodation. This would be an era in which the black bourgeoisie would enjoy the fruits of the civil rights movement while a larger body of "unqualified" Negroes remained segregated and deprived until the next renewal of the Negro's struggle for equality.

• Gradualism Revisited

In addition to the doubt of whether a radical program of political and economic reform would be supported by the white majority, there was the question of whether it would gain the support of Negroes themselves. Gradualism is an inherent feature of a program of building a viable political coalition and then reforming a society through social engineering. Maximizing voter registration, winning victories at the polls, and then translating votes into policy is a tedious, often discouraging task lacking the drama of a demonstration.[9] It is questionable whether Negroes could be mobilized for the long pull required to make them a decisive political power in the nation. Victories would not be quick and sure and setbacks, such as those encountered in the November elections of 1966, would be recurrent. Even if an effective progressive coalition could be forged, the task of reshaping the economic order could be accomplished neither easily nor quickly within the framework of the American political structure. The system of checks and balances, horizontal and vertical, that has always emasculated bold, comprehensive programs of social reform would still operate to frustrate the grand designs of the social planners and to disillusion Negroes who place their faith in such programs. Most important, the shift of the Negro's struggle from protest to politics and then to social engineering would offer little hope of providing that sense of identity that he is still struggling desperately to achieve. It may be argued that during the first decade of demonstrations it has been the struggle itself that has sustained Negroes, not the token victories they have achieved. To suspend the protest in the hope that more significant victories would thereby be achieved in a remote future would be to deprive Negroes of their chief source of pride in the present time.

· Negro Pride and the New Nationalism

It is to this emergent pride that the revolutionary alternative offered by the new radicals, the advocates of Black Power, appeals. It is the same sort of appeal offered by an earlier generation of new radicals when, beginning in 1956, they led Negroes into the streets in demonstrations rather than wait on the result of the long, unsatisfying, legalistic strategy of the NAACP. Not a diminution of conflict and tension, but an intensification of the struggle has always been the answer of the radicals to the impasses the Negro Revolution has seemed to meet. But this latest version of Negro radicalism is the most revolutionary that has appeared. It is defined by white Americans and even by erstwhile radical Negro leaders as unrespectable and revolutionary. This definition is accepted as valid by the new radicals; they make no obeisances to the idols of national unity, legalism, and nonviolence. Instead of a strategy of coalition politics within the framework of a two party system, they propose the creation of a black political party. The suggestion has even been advanced that the black ghettoes become separate cities within the metropolitan areas where they are located. Instead of the preparation of Negroes for integration into a prosperous and presumably expanding white economy, the creation of a parallel Negro economy and the expulsion of white capitalists from the ghettoes has been recommended. Most notably, an appeal to the white man's fear rather than to his love or his guilt is the underlying theme of Black Power. This theme is couched in terms of self-defense, but included in it is a total rejection of the white man's law. Stokely Carmichael made clear his rejection of white America and of its laws when he said:

> We can't be expected any more to march and get our heads broken to say to you that you are nice guys. You are not nice guys. We have found you out. You are rotten through and through, and that's what we are saying. And, Alexander the Great was really Alexander the Barbaric, and that's what we're going to start from.[10]
>
> I've had so much law and order, I swear before God I want some chaos! I want some chaos so bad I can taste it on the tip of my lips, because all I see is law and order everywhere I go. Law and order: from Canton, Mississippi to Watts Los Angeles, to Harlem, to Chicago—nothing but law and order.[11]

Carmichael and SNCC are not the only new radicals to put their foot upon the path of black nationalism. With the election of Floyd McKissick as its leader, traditionally nonviolent CORE assumed a posture that could scarcely be distinguished from that of SNCC. The words written by James Farmer shortly before he left the leadership of CORE presaged this decision to continue the struggle without dependence on white allies or white love. Farmer spoke of a new "mood ebony" in CORE and explained it on the basis of three reasons. First, he spoke of the pride that had developed among Negroes through the achievements of the civil rights movement, saying, "We learned that what was needed was not *invisibility* but a valid and legitimate *visibility*." Second, he spoke of the influence of the masses of black people who were attracted to the banner of CORE. He said, "The integration-which-would-end-in-assimilation has never been a prime goal of the Negro masses. . . . Garveyism remains latent in the Negro ghetto, as our new recruits taught us." Finally, and most significantly, he declared, "The present day black nationalist groups . . . and figures like the late Malcolm X have influenced us perceptibly." [12] Then he advanced the psychological justification for the new strategy of black nationalism, saying:

> Like the nationalists, we must try to conquer the Negro sense of inferiority. We feel this will be possible only when it is legitimate to be a black man in this country. And here CORE has a unique contribution to make. *CORE knows that Negro identity will emerge only in the midst of purposive and realistic effort in America. The nationalists offer doctrine. We must offer program as well.*[13]

Farmer proposed that CORE stick to its "proven techniques of nonviolent direct action." While he had praise for the Deacons for Defense and Justice, he saw more danger than advantage in Malcolm X's bolder doctrine of violence. But McKissick, Carmichael, Brown, and even more so the host of unheralded local Negro leaders who amass arsenals of small arms and Molotov cocktails in the ghettoes, apparently do not share Farmer's fear of a race war.

The prospects for the success of the appeal of the new radicals in producing a large following and drastically changing the structure of American society must be considered from three perspectives. The first considers the sort of psychological appeal that the spirit of total war against white society might have, particularly for the younger generation of Negroes. The second considers the societal conditions that might accentuate Negro impatience and enhance the appeal of the black nationalists. The third perspective requires an examination of the program that may be dimly discerned in the Black Power movement.

· The Appeal of Conflict

Peaceful, secure men usually look at conflict, particularly violent conflict, from a strictly utilitarian standpoint. Unless they are paci- fists, they view conflict as a necessary evil that must always be justified in terms of achieving some greater good. Thus it is as- sumed that the conflict in which rational men will engage will be directed at an enemy who is responsible for the conditions that the aggressors desire to have corrected and that victory will have some logical chance of changing these conditions. Conflict that seems to have no such chance is seen as the blind striking out of irrational, frustrated people who, in their desperation, think not of the conse- quences of their actions. This sort of conflict would seem to serve no function for the participants beyond a temporary release of ten- sion.

It is this sort of thinking that leads to warnings that an intensifi- cation of the Negro's struggle for identity and equality will only serve to bring down the wrath of a powerful white community upon the heads of Negroes. There is another theory that holds that seemingly hopeless conflict has value both for the individuals who participate in it and for the group of which they are a part. The gains for the individual and the group are much greater than mere relief of tension. This doctrine holds that a prideful group identity must be achieved through the birth pangs of conflict. It has been enunciated by the Algerian revolutionist Frantz Fanon in his book *The Wretched of the Earth*.[14] Although the book is about the colonized people of the African continent, many similarities may be found between the plight of the Negro masses in America and that of the native peoples of Africa. Fanon argues that only by taking up arms against the European powers in a total and violent struggle can the peoples of the Third World achieve national identities, national cultures, and national pride. In the preface to Fanon's book, Jean Paul Sartre says:

> He shows clearly that this irrepressible violence is neither sound and fury, nor the resurrection of savage instincts, nor even the effect of resentment: it is man recreating himself. . . . The native cures himself of colonial neurosis by thrusting out the settler through force of arms. When his rage boils over, he rediscovers his lost innocence and he comes to know himself in that he himself creates his self. . . . The rebel's weapon is the proof of his humanity. For in the first days of the revolt you must kill: to shoot down a European is to kill two birds with one stone, to destroy an oppressor and the man he oppresses at the same time: there remains a dead man and a free man; the survivor, for the first time, feels a *national* soil under his foot.[15]

Fanon explains how in his view the struggle to achieve nationhood is an essential ingredient of group consciousness and group unity. He says:

But it so happens that for the colonized people this violence, because it constitutes their only work, invests their characters with positive and creative qualities. The purpose of violence binds them together as a whole, since each individual forms a violent link in the great chain, a part of the great organism of violence which has surged upward in recognition of the settler's violence in the beginning. The groups recognize each other and the future nation is already indivisible. The armed struggle mobilizes the people; that is to say, it throws them in one way and in one direction.

The mobilization of the masses, when it rises out of the war of liberation, introduces into each man's consciousness the ideas of a common cause, of a national destiny and of a collective history. In the same way the second phase, that of the building-up of the nation, is helped on by the existence of this cement which has been mixed with blood and anger. Thus we come to a full appreciation of the originality of the words used in these under-developed countries. During the colonial period the people are called upon to fight against oppression; after national liberation, they are called upon to fight against poverty, illiteracy, and under-development. The struggle, they say, goes on. The people realize that life is an unending contest.[16]

The new radicals of the Negro Revolution, in contrast to strategists such as Bayard Rustin and A. Philip Randolph, are following this philosophy in placing Black Power at the top of the agenda and the war on cultural deprivation at the bottom. They would no longer have Negro Americans come as supplicants seeking the crumbs from the white man's table, ever conscious of their own inferiority. Like Fanon, they argue that pride and a sense of peoplehood must be achieved first if the black man is to enjoy real equality in a society that heretofore has condemned him to inferiority simply on the basis of his blackness. Carmichael speaks of the need of Negro Americans to overcome their own feelings of inferiority when he says:

Black people in this country have to move to a position of psychological equality and that is very, very important. And they can't do that with white people getting everything for them. They have to confront the white power structure themselves, so that means that white allies will have to be pushed aside; we can no longer have white people getting poverty money for you—you have to get it yourself so that you know black people can do those things on their own—so that they don't always need somebody white to do it for them.[17]

One of the charges most frequently thrown at Negro Americans is that having lost their native African culture in slavery they have developed no culture of their own of which they could be proud. The whole notion of cultural pluralism implies that within the framework of the white man's society Negroes should learn to develop and take pride in their own cultural forms. These should be more than pale, shoddy imitations of the white man's culture. Fanon addresses himself indirectly to this notion also. Speaking of the development of national cultures in the emergent nations of Africa, he says:

A frequent mistake, and one which is moreover hardly justifiable is to try to find cultural expressions for and to give new values to native culture within the framework of colonial domination. This is why we arrive at a proposition which at first sight seems paradoxical: The fact that in a colonized country the most elementary, the most savage and the most undifferentiated nationalism is the most fervent and efficient means of defending national culture. . . . The nation is not only the condition of culture, its fruitfulness, its continuous renewal, and its deepening. It is also a necessity. It is the fight for national existence which sets culture moving and opens to it the doors of creation. Later on it is the nation which will insure the conditions and framework necessary to culture.[18]

By the same token, it may be argued that a meaningful and satisfying Negro culture can come into existence in a pluralistic American society only through an antecedent state of black nationalism. In turn, it is through the myth of Black Power that the new radicals are attempting to create this black nationalism.

This is the logic of Black Power as this philosophy might be seen through the eyes of one who views Negro Americans as a colonial people and who has lost all faith in the willingness of white America to grant him real equality. Certainly there are individual black leaders, some enjoying national notoriety, others known only within their own ghetto neighborhoods, who have accepted the major part of this philosophy. By their logic, Watts, Newark, and Detroit were not senseless tragedies of nonrealistic conflict but minor victories in the war by black Americans to achieve identity.

The next phase of the racial crisis will consist of a contest between such leaders and more moderate Negro leaders, such as Martin Luther King, Jr., for the allegiance of the activists within the Negro population. How big a following the new radicals can attract, both to a compact, organized hard core and to a diffuse reserve of adherents who will jump into the fray whenever violence breaks out, will depend upon changes in the social and economic context.

· Economic Factors

One development that would increase the number of desperate Negroes who would be responsive to this doctrine of disillusionment would be a further deterioration of the economic situation of the Negro masses. Continued inflation combined with a lag in the wage scales of unorganized workers and in welfare stipends would have this effect. Even greater economic cramp would be produced, and more quickly, by an economic recession. Even in a period of unprecedented affluence for the society as a whole unemployment among Negroes, particularly young people, remains alarmingly high. For the ghetto youth for whom James Baldwin, LeRoi Jones, and Claude Brown attempt to speak, depression conditions already exist. Were a cutback in employment added to the effects of automation, the army of potential revolutionary fighters would be augmented rapidly. But in another depression it would not be communism, Buy Black campaigns, or the Double Duty Dollar that would beckon to Negroes; it would be Black Power.

One event that could lead to a drastic economic readjustment in the United States would be a return to a peace economy as a result of American disengagement in Viet Nam. Were a reduction in military spending followed quickly by a shift of federal funds to the Freedom Budget, the utopian dream of Rustin and Randolph might be realized and the Negro Revolution terminated peacefully. If this did not happen, however, the end of the Viet Nam war might set the stage for the most violent phase of the Negro Revolution.

· The War in Viet Nam and the Negro Revolution

Many students of revolution have emphasized the close relationship between the involvement of a nation in an external war and the occurrence of a revolution. Chalmers Johnson proposes the term "accelerator" to designate an occurrence that catalyzes or throws into relief "the already existing revolutionary level of dysfunctions." Accelerators "do not of themselves cause revolution; but when they do occur in a system already bearing the necessary level of dysfunction . . . they will provide the sufficient cause of the immediately following revolution." [19]

Johnson identifies defeat in a foreign war as one of the most potent accelerators, noting, "Defeat in war, as an accelerator, shatters the myth of sovereignty, exacts sacrifices—even the supreme sacrifice—from a society's members for an unpopular system, and completes the crippling of an already creaking system; most important, it opens the doors to revolution because of its effects on the army." [20]

It is difficult to speculate about the relationship between the Negro Revolution, which so few Americans recognize as a real revolution, and the Viet Nam war, which officially is not a war! Analysis of the potential relationship between these two rests upon the assumption that there *is* a revolutionary situation in the United States and that the nation *is* engaged in a war, one in which defeat is possible. The analysis is complicated further by the fact that the American army in the field in Viet Nam is the most thoroughly integrated force in United States history; yet it is fighting an enemy that is "colored" and, like the Negro masses in the ghettoes, poor. The Negro leaders most disenchanted with the American society have been quick to point this out.

American withdrawal from Viet Nam, if followed by a final victory for Ho Chi Minh, would constitute a military defeat for the United States, even though the divisions returned intact. It would appear that the United States, although still on its feet, had conceded a technical knockout after challenging Asian communism. Belief in the invincibility of the white hope of the West would be shaken, not only among other nations and peoples but perhaps among Americans themselves, including Negro Americans. The lives lost in battle, including a disproportionate number of Negro lives, would appear to have been sacrificed in vain. To the most alienated Negroes, the altar on which these black soldiers would have been sacrificed would be the white American's vain belief in white supremacy in world affairs.

Chalmers Johnson argues that it is the crippling effect on the army itself, making it an inadequate instrument for defense of the status quo, that makes defeat in war important as an accelerator.

There are no indications that the regular army that might be retained after a reduction of overseas commitments would become an active or even passive abettor of revolutionary violence. It is more likely that the armed forces would remain a bulwark against the *success* of a revolution. But the citizen soldiers, those members of the wartime armed forces who are rapidly demobilized at the conclusion of hostilities, could very well be the precipitant for violent revolution. It is significant that all ten of the founders of the Deacons for Defense and Justice were veterans of Korea or World War II.[21]

Negro veterans might find that they had exchanged the deprivations of the battlefield for the poverty and the indignities of the ghetto. But these would be the most battle-hardened, heroic group of Negroes who had ever fought for America simply because they had been given the greatest opportunity for combat and heroism. Trained, battle-tested, and embittered they could be the source of the guerrilla army that a Negro leader would need for the task of disrupting an American society from which he was totally alienated. Thus any end of massive United States military involvement in Viet Nam, even one coming as a result of token victory, could serve as an accelerator for the Negro Revolution.

· A Battle Plan for Revolution

But what if RAM (Revolutionary Action Movement) or a more violent version of SNCC did become a rallying point for such an army? By what conceivable tactics could the impoverished denizens of the slums attack the might of the civil police and the armed forces of a rich, powerful, white society?

In Los Angeles, Newark, Cleveland, Detroit, and other cities, ghetto residents have already shown how effectively they can defy the police in what were essentially spontaneous, unorganized uprisings. It is true that these uprisings have been brought under control by military forces. But that in so many cities the National Guard had to be employed to restore order is a tribute to the power of Negro violence. Every time the National Guard has been employed to put down a riot, their intervention represented a victory for the rioters over the civilian police, the normal guardians of social peace in an American city.

Although the urban riots of the 1960s have so far stopped with the destruction of millions of dollars worth of private property and an inordinate drain on municipal and state budgets for the restoration of order, at least one blueprint for more widespread social disruption exists. The author of this blueprint is Robert F. Williams, who has been described as the spiritual godfather of RAM and premier of the African-American government in exile.[22] It is impossible to know just how much of a domestic following Williams has had since his flight from a federal warrant in 1961 led him first to Cuba, and then to Red China. There is no question, however, that his tactical ideas for a violent internal struggle, a minority revolution which could succeed in powerful America, are known and quoted by Negro extremists within the country. His belief that a minority revolution has a chance of succeeding in the United States rests upon his analysis of the vulnerability of American society as it is presently constituted. He says:

> The American society is a highly industrialized complex. A highly industrialized and mechanized system is also a very sensitive one. The more machinery required to serve a community, the greater the incidence of mechanical breakdown. The more dependent a community is on mechanization, the more important it is for the wheels of industry to perpetually turn smoothly. The American mind has been conditioned to think of great calamities, wars, and revolutionary upheavals as taking place on distant soil. Because of the vast upper and middle classes in the U.S.A. that have grown accustomed to

comfortable living, the nation is not psychologically prepared for massive violence and a sudden disruption of the essential agencies of the affluent society. The soft society is highly susceptible to panic.[23]

To produce this mechanical breakdown and generate panic, Williams recommends urban guerrilla tactics reminiscent of the methods used in Budapest during the Hungarian uprising. His brief but detailed description of the weapons and tactics is worth repeating.

The weapons of defense employed by Afro-American freedom fighters must consist of a poor man's arsenal. Gasoline fire bombs (Molotov cocktails), lye or acid bombs (made by injecting lye or acid in the metal end of light bulbs) can be used extensively. During the night hours such weapons thrown from rooftops will make the streets impossible for racist cops to patrol. Hand grenades, bazookas, light mortars, rocket launchers, machine guns, and ammunition can be bought clandestinely from service men anxious to make a fast dollar. Freedom fighters in military camps can be contacted to give instructions on use.

Extensive sabotage is possible. Gas tanks on public vehicles can be choked up with sand. Sugar is also highly effective in gasoline lines. Long nails driven through boards attached with long ends are effective to slow the movement of traffic on congested roads at night. This can cause havoc on turnpikes. Derailing of trains causes panic. Explosive booby traps on police telephone boxes can be employed. High-powered sniper rifles are readily available. Armor piercing bullets will penetrate oil storage tanks from a distance. Phosphorous matches (kitchen matches) placed in airconditioning systems will cause delayed explosions which will destroy expensive buildings. Flame throwers can be manufactured at home. Combat experienced ex-service men can easily solve that problem.[24]

Some of the weapons Williams recommends have already been used in urban riots. Small extremist groups in several American cities have already demonstrated their ability to collect weapons. The continued failure of Congress to pass an effective law controlling the possession and sale of small arms makes the creation of such weapons caches a continuing possibility. Ironically, the National Rifle Association has given as one of its grounds for opposition to such a law the need for citizens to possess arms to defend themselves against mob violence.[25]

· The Need for Leadership

But the mere availability of weapons and individuals desperate enough to use them is not sufficient for launching a revolutionary war. There must be centralized leadership and organization, what Chalmers Johnson has called "a rebel infrastructure" or "autonomous government." [26] Williams concedes this in his explanation of how his own small-scale insurrection in Monroe, North Carolina, in 1957 ended in failure after two days of violence. He said:

> The lesson of Monroe teaches that effective self-defense on the part of brutally oppressed and terrorized people requires massive organization with central coordination. External oppressive forces must not be allowed to relieve the besieged racist terrorists. The forces of the state must be kept under pressure in many places simultaneously. The white supremacy masses must be forced to retreat to their homes in order to give security to their individual families.[27]

There is no question that one reason Negro destructiveness has not reached greater heights is the absence of organization and central coordination. Negro leadership in the United States, much like the leadership of the native fascist movement of the late thirties, is fragmented. It consists of many individual stars who spend as much time competing with one another for eminence as they do in promoting their common cause.

The individual leader or the leadership group who might lead the Negro Revolution into a phase of mass insurrection is not yet discernible. Such a person would have to combine charisma with organizational ability. Had he lived, Malcolm X might have been the type of leader who, with his lieutenants, would have been the nucleus for the building of a revolutionary army. It remains to be seen whether SNCC or CORE will produce a charismatic leader who can effectively challenge Martin Luther King, Jr., in capturing the imagination of large numbers of Negroes. It is doubtful that SNCC will constitute an adequate organizational vehicle because of its self-conscious emphasis on internal democracy.

During the summer of 1967, against the background of the infernos of Newark and Detroit, Black Power advocates began a struggle to achieve coordination. In July a national conference on Black Power brought together in Newark not only the extremist groups, but some members of more conservative civil rights organizations. That there is a Black Power element even in the NAACP was demonstrated by an attempted revolt of a group of Young Turks at the 1967 national convention of the organization. Later in the summer, Black Power forces displayed at least temporary unity and strength in forcing concessions from white delegates of the New Left at the National Conference on New Politics in Chicago. Significantly, James Forman, who had been temporarily eclipsed by Carmichael and Brown as a SNCC leader, came to the forefront again in this convention. Among the other Negro leaders present were King and his lieutenant, Ralph Abernathy, veterans like Forman of the nonviolent, interracial phase of the Negro Revolution.

The spirit of Black Power first welled up out of the ghetto and was enunciated by latecomers to the Negro Revolution, to the dismay of these early leaders. If this spirit of desperation begins to inspire members of the black bourgeoisie, as it is slowly doing, the reservoir of capable leadership will be enlarged. Cool-headed, sophisticated strategists may become available to supplement the efforts of the reckless agitators who now dominate the Black Power forces. Then the Negro Revolution will develop the rebel infrastructure that it now lacks.

The emergence of yet a new strong man of the Negro Revolution depends, however, not just upon the existence of capable leaders. It is also contingent upon the unpredictable occurrence of a dramatic event that might thrust one individual into the limelight. Such an event might create a new hero of a new phase of the Negro Revolution, just as King was propelled into a position of leadership by the drama of the Montgomery protest.

Such a leader, yet unknown, may be waiting in the wings for the incident that will make him the rallying point for the now divided radical Negro leadership. How much of a following would gather around such a strong man depends upon situational factors, both domestic and international. Even as he was denouncing the philosophy of Black Power, Martin Luther King, Jr. described one of the circumstances that might cause large numbers of Negroes to turn away from his relatively moderate and nonviolent leadership. He declared, "The burden now shifts to the municipal, state, and federal authorities and all men in seats of power. If they continue to use our nonviolence as a cushion for complacency, the wrath of those suffering a long chain of abuses will rise. The consequence can well be unmanageable and persistent social disorder and moral disaster." [28]

The desperation of King's appeals for a continued adherence to the tactics of nonviolence seem to suggest that he fears that his own star is setting. At the time his star was clearly rising, it was observed, "Negroes demand of protest leaders constant progress. The combination of long-standing discontent, and a new-found belief in the possibility of change produces a constant state of tension and aggressiveness in the Negro community." [29]

At this time certain situational factors giving the advantage to the more militant Negro leader were identified. One was "the tendency of Negroes and white liberals to lionize the leader who displays aggressiveness and courage in defying the white power structure in his community." A second was, "the nationwide and even worldwide press coverage that such a leader is likely to receive, particularly if his tactics are met by illegal violence or police brutality." Then as now, it was observed that Negro leaders "realize that they must combat the suspicion among their followers that they have sold out to the white community and are permitting themselves to be used to preserve the status quo." [30] Martin Luther King, Jr., must today contend against the same situational forces that brought him to prominence as the greatest Negro leader since Booker T. Washington. The demands for ever greater militance and for constant proof of willingness to defy the white man continue to produce increasingly radical Negro leaders. Today King must defend himself against the charge that he is a modern-day Booker T. Washington whose leadership depends upon his acceptability to the white people. If the demand for militance produces Negro leaders even more militant than King, all omens indicate that such leaders will be advocates of violent, not nonviolent, resistance.

As has been pointed out, continued inflation or the occurrence of an economic recession could enhance the advantage that the new radicals already enjoy in appealing to the Negro masses. Even if American society continues to enjoy its precarious prosperity, such leaders will still have an advantage. Emergency action, not a business-as-usual approach, is required to reduce the frustration that is generated by the problems of race and poverty. It is just such a complacent, business-as-usual philosophy that Negro leaders, both moderate and radical, are already denouncing. The moderate leaders, such as Young, Wilkins, King, and Randolph, show even greater concern about the lack of responsiveness of the American body politic to the great needs than do the new radicals. They realize that they cannot maintain their tenuously held positions of leadership unless the Negro Revolution moves off dead center. The movement took a sudden, but nonviolent, spurt forward in 1960 when the sit-ins resolved the impasse created by the failure of the legal tactics of the NAACP to produce change at a greatly accelerated rate. The next spurt forward might well be in the direction of violence.

· Negro Americans and International Relations

The faith of the new radical leaders and their followers in the desirability and feasibility of more aggressive, violent power tactics will be related also to world affairs. Many of these leaders see the Negro Revolution as part of the rise of the Third World. In the words of Harold Isaacs:

> Negroes accustomed always to feeling the big winds blowing against them now begin to feel the new sensation of having the wind at their backs. . . . Great and important things happening to millions of people all over the world affected what was happening to them and what happened to them had become important to everyone.[31]

Frustrated Negroes are not the only ones, after all, who fear that Western white society is plunging towards some unimaginable hell, but Negroes in America do have their peculiarly equivocal status to resolve in their minds as they contemplate these prospects. Negroes of every estate have at one time or another exulted when some outside force has dealt white America a blow, have seen the Japanese, the Russians, or the Afro-Asians at the U.N. as acting somehow for *us* against *them,* and at every crisis ·in our history for half a century they have had to steady themselves with reminders about which, after all, was which. The deep and abiding identification of Negroes with America that has been maintained despite these feelings has had to persist in the face of a society's deep and abiding refusal to identify itself with Negroes.[32]

Thus the relative strength, prestige, and popularity of the United States in reference to Red China, the Afro-Asian nations, the United Nations, the emerging nations of Africa and Southeast Asia, and the sometimes democratic, sometimes communistic, revolutionary parties of Latin America, will influence the extent to which Negro Americans are willing to give American society yet another chance to prove its willingness to count them in. Even if the United States can maintain its position of mjlitary might, *sans* popularity, Negro Americans would find it extremely difficult to maintain their identification with a white American fortress standing, like the Union of South Africa, in defiance of a world in which the colored two-thirds of the population play an increasingly influential role.

In 1967, a significant symptom of a possible weakening of Negro identification with what is perceived as an aggressive America appeared in the commitment of Martin Luther King, Jr., to the peace movement. Although his motives were different, King's move brought him closer to the anti-Establishment position of Stokely Carmichael. At the same time, it created a serious rift between King on the one hand, and Whitney Young and Roy Wilkins on the other, further dividing and weakening the moderate element of Negro leadership.

· The Faith of the Anarchist

Barring an all-out war between Communist China and the United States, how could the most optimistic Negro revolutionaries, without prospect of outside aid, hope literally to overthrow the white man's rule? This is the question that logical, cautious men, not revolutionary leaders, might ask. Confident in the faith that, with organization and the tactics of urban guerrilla warfare, they could bring the American social system to a state of chaos, the revolutionary leaders leave to a later date consideration of what sort of social structure could be rebuilt from a disorganized America in which white supremacy had been proven untenable.

One of the major elements which Howard Elinson identifies in the new radical leadership of the Negro Revolution is the new anarchists who, he points out, play an important part in SNCC, and in the Congress of Racial Equality in some areas. The important thing to recognize about the new anarchists and the approach they represent is the *absence* of a program for societal reconstruction. As Elinson says, "The goals and principles of the new anarchists are extremely difficult to describe, partly because the movement is committed to an ideology of nonideology; they are prone to deny that they have any set program." [33] To the extent that a new generation of Negro revolutionary leadership accepts the philosophy of the new anarchists, their concern will be with tearing down the established order, not with devising a new order. The building of a new order would be left to the operation of their ideal of participatory democracy.

· A Race Against Time

The United States is engaged in a dangerous race against time. It is a race against the day that the majority of Negroes decide that the future must be better than the present that white America offers them. The new radicals among Negro leaders are playing an equally dangerous game, however. White America has not reacted to the social disruption and the threats of even greater violence by taking heroic measures to redress the grievances that every Negro leader points to as the basic cause of Negro protests. The demand for integration that dominated the movement for so many years has been met with an ingeniously engineered tokenism, so frustrating as to cause many Negro leaders to abandon integration as a value. The demand for relief of Negro poverty has been met by an antipoverty program that has become bogged down in the morass of patronage and power politics. This program now is threatened with retrenchment because of a popular demand to hold the line of federal expenditures while still maintaining the military efforts in Viet Nam. Hence, the warnings of continued and greater violence to come are likely to be fulfilled. The warning of de Tocqueville, voiced over a century ago, remains both timely and ominous:

> If ever the free institutions of America are destroyed, that event may be attributed to the unlimited authority of the majority, which may at some future time urge the minorities to desperation, and oblige them to have recourse to physical force. Anarchy will then be the result, but it will have been brought about by despotism.[34]

There is every indication that the white electorate and its elected representatives will react to continued threats and to more violence in the streets not by a renewed effort to understand and alleviate the plight of underprivileged Negroes, but by reactionary measures to suppress these disorders. Given a choice between a massive freedom budget and a police state, the American electorate is more likely to choose the latter. The tide may have turned in the direction of a police state when, in the Eighty-ninth Congress, the

House of Representatives passed the so-called antiriot amendment to the civil rights bill while failing to pass the bill itself. Moynihan saw in the results of the elections of November, 1966, "a bruising declaration that the electorate is fed up to the teeth with demonstrations and riots. . . ." [35]

The simple truth, too often overlooked in optimistic analyses of the racial crisis in America, is that neither white nor black Americans are a breed of angels. They are not set aside from the people of other nations and other tribes by superior rationality or greater tenderness toward one another. Despite repeated exposés of the organization's utter perversion of Christianity and Americanism, white Americans have allowed the Ku Klux Klan to rise again and again to the point where it could terrorize whole communities. Less than twenty years ago, McCarthyism put the nation into battle against an enemy whose visibility was far less than that of the forthright, defiant black extremists of the present day. In the hardcore states of the Deep South, racist politicians still find it politically profitable to run on platforms proposing to turn back the clock of race relations, not just to stop further progress. In the city of Chicago, in the summer of 1966, white Americans responded to Martin Luther King's latest campaign of nonviolence by shouting "white power" and contributing to the war chest of the late George Lincoln Rockwell's American Nazi party.

During the nonviolent phase of the Negro Revolution the majority of those white Americans who pride themselves on their Christian love have found it difficult to extend this love to Martin Luther King, Jr., and the middle-class Negro youth of the sit-ins and the picket lines. In the future, they will face the ultimate challenge to their capacity for Christ-like love as they are confronted by Negro leaders who talk of hate, not love, for the white man, and by the unlovely publicans and sinners of the Negro lower class. There is no assurance that the commitment of the majority of white Americans to democratic values and the forgiving spirit of Christ can stand the challenge of Black Power.

Nor is there assurance that Negro Americans will accept the verdict of logic that a Negro Revolution is, indeed, impossible in twentieth-century America. How much longer will they settle for whatever white Americans are willing to give them? From the lips of a traditional hero of white America, they have the battle cry, "Give me liberty or give me death!" They have their own heroes in Nat Turner, Denmark Vesey, and Harriet Tubman, and even in the street fighters of Detroit, Newark, and Watts. The new radical leaders can point to the failure of the conciliatory strategy of Booker T. Washington and Martin Luther King, Jr., to achieve the goal of freedom for Negroes. They can couch their own appeals in terms of a return to the strategy of power advocated by Frederick Douglass and W. E. B. DuBois. Even faced with the possibility of a fascist America dedicated to preventing Negroes from achieving their goals regardless of the cost to American democracy, they can harken to the yet unheeded appeal of Claude McKay, voiced in the thirties:[36]

> If we must die, let it not be like hogs,
> Hunted and penned in an inglorious spot,
> While round us bark the mad and hungry dogs,
> Making their mock at our accursed lot.
> If we must die, O let us nobly die,
> So that our precious blood may not be shed
> In vain; then even the monsters we defy
> Shall be constrained to honor us though dead!
> O Kinsman! We must meet the common foe!
> Though far outnumbered let us show us brave,
> And for their thousand blows deal one death blow!
> What though before us lies the open grave?

Like men we'll face the murderous, cowardly pack,
Pressed to the wall, dying, but fighting back!

Assessment of the countervailing power that the white Establishment could muster to oppose even the best organized revolution of Black Power makes the Negro Revolution seem indeed to be the Impossible Revolution. That such a revolution might be attempted in the face of overwhelming odds and without regard to the terrible consequences is not at all impossible.

Notes

Chapter I

1. Louis Lomax, *The Negro Revolt* (New York: Harper & Row, 1962).
2. William Brink and Louis Harris, *The Negro Revolution in America* (New York: Simon and Schuster, 1964).
3. Robert Penn Warren, *Who Speaks for the Negro* (New York: Vintage Books, 1966).
4. *Ibid.*, p. 151.
5. *Ibid.*, p. 218.
6. Whitney Young, Jr., *To Be Equal* (New York: McGraw-Hill, 1964), p. 239.
7. James Farmer, "The New Jacobins and Full Emancipation," in Robert A. Goldwin, ed., *100 Years of Emancipation* (Chicago: Rand McNally, 1963), pp. 89–102.
8. *Ibid.*, pp. 95–97.
9. *Ibid.*, p. 99.
10. This definition of revolution is suggested by Crane Brinton, *The Anatomy of Revolution* (New York: Vintage Books, 1957), p. 4.
11. Rex D. Hopper, "The Revolutionary Process: A Frame of Reference for the Study of Revolutionary Movements," *Social Forces*, 28 (March 1950), 270–79.
12. This definition of revolution is based on criteria suggested by Ralph H. Turner and Lewis M. Killian in *Collective Behavior* (Englewood Cliffs, N. J.: Prentice-Hall, 1957), pp. 328–29.
13. Sinclair Lewis, *It Can't Happen Here* (Garden City, N. J.: Sun Dial Press, 1935).
14. George E. Simpson and J. Milton Yinger, *Racial and Cultural Minorities* (New York: Harper & Row, 1965), pp. 534–35.
15. Jane Record and Wilson Record, "Ideological Forces and the Negro Protest," *The Annals* (January 1965), p. 90. See also Seymour M. Lipset, *The First New Nation* (New York: Basic Books, 1963), pp. 340–48.

16. *Ibid.*
17. Robin M. Williams, Jr., "Social Change and Social Conflict: Race Relations in the United States, 1944–1964," *Sociological Inquiry*, 35 (Winter 1965), 8–25.
18. See Leon H. Keyserling, *Progress or Poverty: The U.S. at the Crossroads* (Washington: Conference on Economic Progress, 1964); and Rashi Fein, "An Economic and Social Profile of the Negro American," in Talcott Parsons and Kenneth B. Clark, eds., *The Negro American* (Boston: Houghton Mifflin, 1966), pp. 102–33. See also Michael Harrington, *The Other America: Poverty in the United States* (Baltimore: Penguin Books, 1963).

Chapter II

1. Scott Greer and Peter Orleans, "Political Sociology," in R. E. L. Faris, ed., *Handbook of Modern Sociology* (Chicago: Rand McNally, 1964), p. 841.
2. Alan P. Grimes, *Equality in America* (New York: Oxford University Press, 1964), p. 125.
3. See Milton M. Gordon, *Assimilation in American Life* (New York: Oxford University Press, 1964), Chs. 2 and 3.
4. Grimes, *op. cit.*, p. ix.
5. Will Herberg, *Protestant-Catholic-Jew* (New York: Doubleday, 1955).
6. Ruby Jo Kennedey, "Single or Triple Melting-Pot? Intermarriage Trends in New Haven, 1870–1940," *American Journal of Sociology*, 49 (January 1944), 331–39.
7. Gordon, *op. cit.*
8. Based on unpublished paper by Lee Sloan, "Urban Government and the Politics of Race," delivered at Ohio Valley Sociological Association Meetings, April 27–29, 1967.
9. See Lewis M. Killian, "Community Structure and the Role of the Negro Leader-Agent," *Sociological Inquiry*, 35 (Winter 1965), 69–79.
10. Peter Berger, *The Noise of Solemn Assemblies* (New York: Doubleday, 1961), pp. 40–41. See also Joseph Fichter, "American Religion and the Negro," in Talcott Parsons and Kenneth B. Clark, eds., *The Negro American* (Boston: Houghton Mifflin, 1966), pp. 401–07.
11. *Ibid.*, p. 116.
12. Frank Tannenbaum, *Slave and Citizen* (New York: Alfred A. Knopf, 1947).
13. Grimes, *op. cit.*, p. 41.
14. Quoted in George Livermore, *The Opinions of the Founders of the Republic on Negroes as Slaves, as Citizens, and as Soldiers* (Boston: A. Williams, 1963), p. 18.

15. Harry V. Jaffa, "The Emancipation Proclamation," in Robert A. Goldwin, ed., *100 Years of Emancipation* (Chicago: Rand McNally, 1963), p. 15.
16. *Ibid.*, p. 23.
17. Frederick Douglass, *Life and Times of Frederick Douglass* (New York: Collier Books, 1962), p. 217.
18. *Ibid.*
19. *Ibid.*, p. 378.
20. *Ibid.*, p. 379.
21. Benjamin Quarles, *Frederick Douglass* (Washington: The Associated Publishers, 1948), pp. 224–25.
22. Douglass, *op. cit.*, p. 539.
23. *Ibid.*
24. See Wilson Record, *Race and Radicalism: The NAACP and the Communist Party in Conflict* (Ithaca: Cornell University Press, 1964), pp. 55–57, 138–39, and 220.
25. In *Buchanan v. Worley*, the U.S. Supreme Court declared unconstitutional a Louisville, Kentucky, zoning ordinance designed to segregate Negroes. In the Gaines case, the court ruled that requiring a Negro to accept a state-provided tuition scholarship and to go to a law school in another state violated the equal protection clause of the Fourteenth Amendment since a law school for white students was provided within the state. NAACP attorneys successfully pleaded both of these cases.

Chapter III

1. Appendix A, *Amicus curiae* brief of the Attorney General of Florida, in the case of *Oliver Brown, et al., v. Board of Education of Topeka, Kansas,* in the Supreme Court of the United States, October term, 1954.
2. Louis Lomax, *The Negro Revolt* (New York: Harper & Row, 1962), pp. 84–85.
3. Leonard Broom and Norval Glenn, *Transformation of the Negro American* (New York: Harper & Row, 1965), p. 8.
4. Quoted by Ralph McGill in "W. E. B. DuBois," *The Atlantic* (November 1965), p. 79.
5. Gunnar Myrdal, *An American Dilemma* (New York: Harper and Brothers, 1944), p. 741.
6. Lomax, *op. cit.*, p. 206.
7. Warren D. St. James, *The National Association for the Advancement of Colored People: A Case Study in Pressure Groups* (New York: Exposition Press, 1958), p. 116.
8. Myrdal, *op. cit.*, p. 830.

9. William Brink and Louis Harris, *The Negro Revolution in America* (New York: Simon and Schuster, 1964), pp. 116–17.
10. *Ibid.*
11. *Ibid.*, p. 124.
12. Lerone Bennett, Jr., *The Negro Mood* (New York: Ballantine Books, 1964), p. 40.
13. Jack Greenberg, "The Role of Law in Fulfilling These Rights," Background Paper for White House Preliminary Planning Conference, "To Fulfill These Rights" (November 1965), p. 8.
14. Crane Brinton, *The Anatomy of Revolution* (New York: Vintage Books, 1957), pp. 44–52.
15. Ernest Q. Campbell and Thomas F. Pettigrew, *Christians in Racial Crisis* (Washington: Public Affairs Press, 1959).
16. Joseph Fichter, "American Religion and the Negro," in Talcott Parsons and Kenneth B. Clark, eds., *The Negro American* (Boston: Houghton Mifflin, 1966), pp. 415–16.
17. Quoted in Lomax, *op. cit.*, p. 94.
18. Campbell and Pettigrew, *op. cit.*, pp. 156–59.
19. Fichter, *op. cit.*, p. 410.
20. Brinton, *op. cit.*, p. 50.
21. Milton M. Gordon, *Assimilation in American Life* (New York: Oxford University Press, 1964), p. 9.
22. Lomax, *op. cit.*, p. 102.
23. George S. Pettee, *The Process of Revolution* (New York: Harper and Brothers, 1938), p. 33.
24. *Ibid.*, p. 32.
25. Bayard Rustin, "From Protest to Politics: The Future of the Civil Rights Movement," *Commentary* (February 1965), p. 1.
26. Pettee, *op. cit.*, p. 61.
27. James Vander Zanden, *Race Relations in Transition* (New York: Random House, 1965), p. 99.
28. The term "myth" is used in the sense suggested by Georges Sorel, the French Syndicalist of the early part of the twentieth century. He used the concept myth to designate a vision of the future that, no matter how impractical and utopian it might seem in the light of reason, inspires men to act on the present. Whether the myth might ever come to pass is unimportant, Sorel contended; it is the revolutionary sentiments and the desperate actions that it evokes in those who believe it that are important. See Georges Sorel, *Reflections on Violence*, trans., T. E. Hulme and J. Roth (Glencoe, Ill.: The Free Press, 1950), pp. 142–47.
29. Brink and Harris, *op. cit.*, p. 145.

Chapter IV

1. James Vander Zanden, *Race Relations in Transition* (New York: Random House, 1965), p. 87.
2. John A. Morsell, "Legislation and Its Implementation," *Journal of Negro Education*, Vol. 34 (Summer 1965), p. 232.
3. George E. Simpson and J. Milton Yinger, *Racial and Cultural Minorities* (New York: Harper & Row, 1965), p. 421.
4. Vincent Harding, "Where Have All the Lovers Gone?," *New South*, Vol. 21 (Winter 1966), p. 29.
5. Vander Zanden, *op. cit.*, p. 90.
6. *Ibid.*, p. 92.
7. Richard Walton, "Two Strategies of Social Change and Their Dilemmas" (Institute Paper No. 95, Purdue University, Institute for Research in the Behavioral, Economical, Management Sciences, December 1964).
8. Quoted in Robert F. Williams, *Negroes With Guns* (New York: Marzani and Munsell, 1962), p. 14.
9. Walton, *op. cit.*, p. 15.
10. James Q. Wilson, "The Strategy of Protest: Problems of Negro Civic Action," *Journal of Conflict Resolution*, Vol. 5 (September 1961), p. 291.
11. Based on an analysis by Robert M. White, "The Tallahassee Sit-Ins and CORE: A Nonviolent Revolutionary Submovement" (unpublished Ph.D. dissertation, The Florida State University, Tallahassee, Florida, 1964), Ch. 3.
12. Wilson, *op. cit.*, p. 292.
13. David H. Bayley, "The Pedagogy of Democracy: Coercive Public Protest in India," *American Political Science Review*, Vol. 56 (September 1962), pp. 663–72.
14. *Ibid.*, p. 663.
15. *Ibid.*, p. 665.
16. *Ibid.*
17. Quoted in Alan F. Westin, ed., *Freedom Now* (New York: Basic Books, 1964), p. 39.
18. Louis Lomax, *The Negro Revolt* (New York: Harper & Row, 1962), p. 86.
19. Mel Elfin, "Why Pick on New Rochelle?," *The Reporter* (December 8, 1960), pp. 28–30.
20. Harding, *op. cit.*, p. 31.
21. Martin Luther King, Jr., *Why We Can't Wait* (New York: Harper & Row, 1963), p. 157.
22. *Ibid.*, p. 92.

23. *Ibid.*, p. 7.
24. Lerone Bennett, Jr., *The Negro Mood* (New York: Ballantine Books, 1964), p. 23.
25. King, *op. cit.*, p. 128.
26. Bayard Rustin, "From Protest to Politics: The Future of the Civil Rights Movement," *Commentary* (February 1965), p. 30.
27. *Ibid.*, p. 25.
28. Louis Lomax, "The White Liberal," *Ebony* (August 1965), p. 62.
29. Crane Brinton, *The Anatomy of Revolution* (New York: Vintage Books, 1957), pp. 128–30.
30. Rustin, *op. cit.*, p. 29.
31. Brinton, *op. cit.*, pp. 146–47.
32. Simeon Booker, "The Great Society," *Ebony* (August 1965), pp. 149–53.
33. Rustin, *op. cit.*, p. 29.
34. William S. Schirer, *The Rise and Fall of the Third Reich* (New York: Simon and Schuster, 1960), p. 135.
35. William Brink and Louis Harris, *The Negro Revolution in America* (New York: Simon and Schuster, 1964), p. 142.
36. *Ibid.*, p. 145.
37. *Ibid.*
38. Louis Harris, "Demonstrations New U.S. Doubts," *The Harris Poll* (Washington: The Washington Post, July 12, 1965).
39. Louis Harris, "Freedom Most Valued Asset for Americans," *The Harris Poll* (Washington: The Washington Post, October 25, 1965).
40. Harris, "Demonstrations New U.S. Doubts," *op. cit.*
41. Bayley, *op. cit.*, p. 665.
42. Oscar Handlin, *Firebell in the Night* (Boston: Little, Brown, 1964), p. 67.
43. Charles Silberman, *Crisis in Black and White* (New York: Random House, 1964), p. 8.

Chapter V

1. Quoted in Francis L. Broderick and August Meier, eds., *Negro Protest Thought in the Twentieth Century* (Indianapolis: Bobbs-Merrill, 1965), p. 309.
2. Martin Mayer, "The Shock Troups of the Negro Revolt," *Saturday Evening Post* (November 21, 1964), p. 79.
3. *Ibid.*, pp. 79–80.
4. Quoted in Broderick and Meier, *op. cit.*, p. 422.
5. Alfred McClung Lee and Norman D. Humphrey, *Race Riot* (New York: Dryden Press, 1943), p. 98.

6. James B. Conant, *Slums and Suburbs* (New York: McGraw-Hill, 1961), p. 116.

7. Lewis M. Killian and Charles Grigg, *Racial Crisis in America* (Englewood Cliffs, N. J.: Prentice-Hall, 1964), p. 127.

8. Malcolm X, "I'm Talking to You, White Man," *Saturday Evening Post* (September 12, 1964), p. 53.

9. "What Negroes in the North are Really After," *U.S. News and World Report* (June 10, 1963), p. 40.

10. Robin M. Williams, Jr., "Social Change and Social Conflict: Race Relations in the United States, 1944–1964," *Sociological Inquiry*, 35 (Winter 1965), 20.

11. *Ibid.*, pp. 23–24.

12. Robert Blauner, "Whitewash over Watts," *Trans-Action*, Vol. III (March–April 1966), p. 9.

13. *Ibid.*

14. Leon Trotsky, *The Russian Revolution* (New York: Doubleday, 1959), pp. x–xi.

15. Thomas Pettigrew, "Complexity and Change in American Racial Patterns: A Social Psychological View," in Talcott Parsons and Kenneth B. Clark, eds., *The Negro American* (Boston: Houghton Mifflin, 1966), pp. 352–53.

16. Gunnar Myrdal, *An American Dilemma* (New York: Harper and Brothers, 1944), p. 525.

17. *Ibid.*, p. 528.

18. George Rudé, *The Crowd in History* (New York: John Wiley and Sons, 1964), p. 247.

19. *Ibid.*, pp. 248–49.

20. Quoted in *Newsweek* (August 30, 1965), p. 19.

21. Rudé, *op. cit.*, p. 249.

22. "Protest March Canceled," Los Angeles *Times*, September 3, 1965, p. 3.

23. "Tampa Negro Leaders Warn Bi-Racial Group of Unrest," St. Petersburg *Times*, September 24, 1966, p. 12B.

24. "Black Power, White Backlash," CBS *Reports*, September 27, 1966.

25. "San Francisco Tensely Calm," St. Petersburg *Times*, September 30, 1966, p. 1A.

26. "Police Hearing Boycotted by Rights Groups," Los Angeles *Times*, June 11, 1966, Part I, p. 3.

27. Jerry Cohen and William S. Murphy, "There's Still Hell to Pay in Watts," *Life* (July 15, 1966), p. 63.

28. Frederick Douglass, *Life and Times of Frederick Douglass* (New York: Collier Books, 1962), p. 539.

29. Daniel P. Moynihan, *The Negro Family: The Case for National Action* (Washington: U.S. Government Printing Office, 1965).

30. Lee Rainwater and William Yancey, "Black Families and the White House," *Trans-Action*, Vol. III (July–August 1966), pp. 6–11, 48–53. For a fuller treatment, see Rainwater and Yancey, *The Moynihan Report and the Politics of Controversy* (Cambridge: The M.I.T. Press, 1967).

31. "A CORE Charge to the White House Conference" (mimeographed, November 17–18, 1965).

32. See Daniel P. Moynihan, "The President and the Negro: The Moment Lost," *Commentary* (February 1967), pp. 31–45.

33. "A CORE Charge to the White House Conference," *op. cit.*

34. Moynihan, "The President and the Negro," *op. cit.*, p. 39.

35. "SNCC Snubs Johnson Bid to Rights Session," Los Angeles *Times*, May 24, 1966, Part I, p. 16.

36. *Ibid.*

37. *Ibid.*

38. Rainwater and Yancey, *op. cit.*, p. 53.

39. Quoted in Howard Zinn, *SNCC, The New Abolitionists* (Boston: Beacon Press, 1964), p. 215.

40. Martin Luther King, Jr., *Why We Can't Wait* (New York: Harper & Row, 1963), p. 57.

41. Rainwater and Yancey, *op. cit.*, p. 53.

42. Howard Elinson, "Radicalism and the Negro Movement," in Raymond J. Murphy and Howard Elinson, eds., *Problems and Prospects of the Negro Movement* (Belmont, Calif.: Wadsworth, 1966), p. 356.

Chapter VI

1. James H. Hargett, "Negroes and Leadership," Los Angeles *Times*, March 26, 1966, Part III, p. 4. Quoted by permission of the publishers.

2. Pat Watters, *Encounter With the Future* (Atlanta: Southern Regional Council, 1965), p. 1.

3. Harold Isaacs, "Integration and the Negro Mood," *Commentary* (December 1962), p. 494.

4. Samuel Dubois Cook, "The Tragic Myth of Black Power," *New South*, 21 (Summer 1966), 59.

5. Bruce Detwiler, "A Time to be Black," *New Republic* (September 17, 1966), p. 19.

6. Cook, *op. cit.*, p. 60.

7. Lewis M. Killian and Charles Grigg, *Racial Crisis in America* (Englewood Cliffs, N. J.: Prentice-Hall, 1964), p. 106.

8. J. Michael Ross, Thomas Crawford, and Thomas Pettigrew, "Negro Neighbors—Banned in Boston," *Trans-Action*, Vol. III (September–October, 1966), pp. 13–18.

9. *Ibid.*, p. 15.

10. *Ibid.*

11. David Danzig, "The Meaning of Negro Strategy," *Commentary* (February 1964), pp. 42–43.

12. Ross *et al., op. cit.*, p. 16.

13. See Milton Himmelfarb, "Negroes, Jews, and Muzhiks," *Commentary* (October 1966), pp. 83–86.

14. "White Backlash Worrying Labor," Tampa *Tribune*, October 26, 1966, p. 6A.

15. David Danzig, "Rightists, Racists, and Separatists: A White Bloc in the Making?," *Commentary* (August 1964), p. 30.

16. Nathan Glazer, "Negroes and Jews: The New Challenge to Pluralism," *Commentary* (December 1964), pp. 33–34.

17. Nathan Glazer and Daniel Moynihan, *Beyond the Melting Pot* (Cambridge: The M.I.T. Press, 1963), pp. 99–110.

18. L. Singer, "Ethnogenesis and Negro-Americans Today," *Social Research*, Vol. 29 (Winter 1962), p. 429.

19. *Ibid.*, pp. 430–31.

20. Georges Sorel, *Reflections on Violence*, trans. T. E. Hulme and J. Roth (Glencoe, Ill.: The Free Press, 1950), pp. 124–26.

21. *The New York Times*, August 5, 1966, p. 1.

22. "What We Want," *The New York Review of Books*, September 22, 1966, p. 5.

23. *Ibid.*

24. *Ibid.*, p. 6.

25. David Danzig, "In Defense of Black Power," *Commentary* (September 1966), pp. 44–45.

26. "What We Want," *op. cit.*, pp. 6–7.

27. *Ibid.*, p. 6.

28. Howard Elinson, "Radicalism and the Negro Movement," in Raymond J. Murphy and Howard Elinson, eds., *Problems and Prospects of the Negro Movement* (Belmont, Calif.: Wadsworth, 1966), p. 370.

29. "What We Want," *op. cit.*, p. 6.

30. Quoted in St. Petersburg *Times*, April 19, 1967, p. 3.

Chapter VII

1. Whitney Young, Jr., *To Be Equal* (New York: McGraw-Hill, 1964), p. 247.

2. James Farmer, *Freedom—When?* (New York: Random House, 1965), p. 170.

3. Bayard Rustin, "From Protest to Politics: The Future of the Civil Rights Movement," *Commentary* (February 1965), p. 28.

4. *Ibid.*

5. *Ibid.*, p. 27.

6. Sidney Wilhelm and Elwin Powell, "Who Needs the Negro?," *Trans-Action*, Vol. I (September–October, 1964), p. 6.

7. *Ibid.*

8. Daniel P. Moynihan, "The President and the Negro: The Moment Lost," *Commentary* (February 1967), p. 31.

9. See Donald R. Matthews and James W. Prothro, *Negroes and the New Southern Politics* (New York: Harcourt, Brace & World, 1966).

10. Stokely Carmichael, "Black Power: The Widening Dialogue," *New South*, Vol. 21 (Summer 1966), p. 67.

11. *Ibid.*, p. 76.

12. Farmer, *op. cit.*, p. 92–93.

13. *Ibid.*, p. 106.

14. Frantz Fanon, *The Wretched of the Earth*, trans. Constance Farrington (New York: Grove Press, 1963), p. 10. Quotations used by permission of the publisher.

15. *Ibid.*, pp. 18–19.

16. *Ibid.*, p. 73.

17. Carmichael, *op. cit.*, p. 66.

18. Fanon, *op. cit.*, pp. 196–97.

19. Chalmers Johnson, *Revolution and the Social System* (Stanford: The Hoover Institution on War, Revolution, and Peace, 1964), p. 12.

20. *Ibid.*, p. 14.

21. See Charles C. Moskos, Jr., "Racial Integration in the Armed Forces," *American Journal of Sociology*, Vol. 72 (September 1966), pp. 132–48.

22. See Russell Sackett, "Plotting a War on Whitey," *Life* (June 10, 1966), pp. 101–02.

23. Robert F. Williams, "For Effective Self Defense," in Francis L. Broderick and August Meier, eds., *Negro Protest Thought in the Twentieth Century* (New York: Bobbs-Merrill, 1965), p. 329. Quoted by permission of the publisher.

24. *Ibid.*, p. 331. Quoted by permission of the publisher.

25. "Who Guards America's Homes?" editorial in *The American Rifleman* (May 1967), p. 16.

26. Johnson, *op. cit.*, p. 62.

27. Williams, *op. cit.*, p. 331. Quoted by permission of the publisher.

28. Martin Luther King, Jr., "It is Not Enough to Condemn Black Power," advertisement in *The New York Times*, July 26, 1966.

29. Lewis M. Killian, "Leadership in the Desegregation Crisis: An Institutional Analysis," in Muzafer Sherif, ed., *Intergroup Relations and Leadership* (New York: John Wiley and Sons, 1962), p. 159.

30. *Ibid.*, pp. 160–61.
31. Harold Isaacs, *The New World of Negro Americans* (New York: John Day, 1963), p. 50.
32. *Ibid.*, p. 339.
33. Howard Elinson, "Radicalism and the Negro Movement," in Raymond J. Murphy and Howard Elinson, eds., *Problems and Prospects of the Negro Movement* (Belmont, Calif.: Wadsworth, 1966), p. 361.
34. Alexis de Tocqueville, *Democracy in America*, trans. Henry Reeve (New York: D. Appleton, 1899), Vol. 1, pp. 286–87.
35. Moynihan, *op. cit.*, p. 31.
36. "If We Must Die," in Claude McKay, *Selected Poems of Claude McKay* (New York: Bookman Associates, 1953). Permission to reprint granted by Twayne Publishers.

Selected Readings

BALDWIN, JAMES. *The Fire Next Time.* New York: Dell Publishing Company, 1962.

A now famous enunciation by one of the foremost Negro writers in America of the mood out of which the Black Power philosophy has grown.

BRODERICK, FRANCIS L. and AUGUST MEIER. *Negro Protest Thought in the Twentieth Century.* Indianapolis: Bobbs-Merrill, 1965.

A collection of writings and statements by Negro leaders from Booker T. Washington through Robert F. Williams, covering the period of accommodation to the era of the new militancy.

BROOM, LEONARD and NORVAL GLENN. *Transformation of the Negro American.* New York: Harper & Row, 1965.

A sociological analysis of the adjustment of Negroes to their position in American society since emancipation. Particularly good for the analysis of the occupation and income of Negro Americans.

BLUMER, HERBERT. "The Future of the Color Line," in John C. McKinney and Edgar T. Thompson, (eds.), *The South in Continuity and Change.* Durham: Duke University Press, 1965.

An examination of the future prospects for race relations in view of the changing nature of the color line as the racial struggle shifts from the South to the urban North. Emphasizes the limitations of formal controls as a means of equalizing the status positions of the two racial groups in American society.

CLARK, KENNETH B. *Dark Ghetto: Dilemmas of Social Power.* New York: Harper & Row, 1965.

A study based on observations in the Harlem ghetto, interpreting the psychology of the ghetto and the ambivalent relationship between the Negro and the white liberal.

DANZIG, DAVID. "In Defense of Black Power." *Commentary,* September 1966, pp. 41–46.

A white sociologist argues that the Black Power theme is the answer to the ineffectiveness of the liberal coalition in meeting both the material and the psychological needs of the Negro masses.

ESSIEN-UDOM, E. U. *Black Nationalism: A Search For an Identity in America.* Chicago: The University of Chicago Press, 1962.

A study of the Black Muslims, including a brief history of the development of the nationalist tradition among Negro Americans. Suggests why integration may be inadequate as a goal for Negro America.

GANS, HERBERT J. *The Urban Villagers.* New York: The Free Press, 1962.

A portrayal of pluralism in modern America based on a study of second generation Italian Americans in Boston.

KILLIAN, LEWIS M. "Social Movements," in R. E. L. Faris (ed.), *Handbook of Modern Sociology.* Chicago: Rand McNally, 1964, pp. 426–55.

A discussion of the types, the properties, the structure, and the development of social movements. Includes a discussion of the development of revolutionary tendencies in social movements.

MEIER, AUGUST and ELLIOTT M. RUDWICK. *From Plantation to Ghetto.* New York: Hill and Wang, 1966.

One of the most recent histories of the Negro in the United States, with particular emphasis upon developments in Negro protest and leadership.

MILLER, HERMAN P. *Rich Man, Poor Man.* New York: Thomas Y. Crowell, 1964.

A detailed but highly readable statistical analysis of the distribution of wealth in modern America. Answers the question, "Who are the poor?" showing particularly the disproportionate impact of poverty on Negroes.

NEWFIELD, JACK. *A Prophetic Minority.* New York: New American Library, 1966.

A description of the development of the new left and an analysis of the various positions represented by its many factions. Particularly valuable for its history of SNCC and the relationship of this organization to other new left groups.

REDDICK, L. D. *Crusader Without Violence.* New York: Harper & Row, 1959.

A brief biography of Martin Luther King, Jr., describing in detail the events surrounding his emergence as a national leader during the Montgomery bus boycott.

RUSTIN, BAYARD. "Black Power and Coalition Politics." *Commentary,* September 1966, pp. 35–40.

A militant Negro leader who objects to the Black Power concept analyzes its effect on the Negro protest movement and pleads for a strategy of coalition policies.

SILBERMAN, CHARLES E. *Crisis in Black and White*. New York: Random House, 1964.

A highly perceptive analysis in which the author foresaw the deepening of the crisis in race relations. One of the first warnings of the shift from preoccupation with segregation in the South to concern for the problems of northern ghettoes.

STRINGFELLOW, WILLIAM. *My People is the Enemy*. New York: Holt, Rinehart and Winston, 1964.

A sensitive and penetrating description of the conditions in Harlem by a white attorney who lived and worked in the ghetto. Emphasizes the estrangement between the races in the North and the potential for violence in the Negro Revolution.

WILL, ROBERT E. and HAROLD B. VATTER. *Poverty in Affluence*. New York: Harcourt, Brace & World, 1965.

A collection of readings on poverty in America, including a critical analysis of governmental programs for the relief of poverty.

WILSON, JAMES Q. *Negro Politics: The Search for Leadership*. New York: The Free Press, 1960.

An analysis of Negro political styles and the effectiveness of Negro politics in the northern city using Chicago as the model.

Index